Dynamic Routing: OSPF, EIGRP and BGP in Cisco, Juniper and Mikrotik

James Relington

DEDICATION

To those who seek knowledge, inspiration, and new perspectives—
may this book be a companion on your journey, a spark for curiosity,
and a reminder that every page turned is a step toward discovery.

DEDICATION

To those who seek knowledge, inspiration, and new perspectives—
may this book be a companion on your journey, a spark for curiosity,
and a reminder that every page turned is a step toward discovery.

AKNOWLEDGEMENTS

I would like to express my deepest gratitude to everyone who contributed to the creation of this book. To my colleagues and mentors, your insights and expertise have been invaluable. A special thank you to my family and friends for their unwavering support and encouragement throughout this journey.

Chapter 1: Introduction to Dynamic Routing

Dynamic routing is a foundational concept in modern networking that enables routers to automatically discover and maintain paths through a network. Unlike static routing, where routes must be manually configured and maintained by a network administrator, dynamic routing protocols allow routers to communicate with each other and dynamically adapt to changes in the network topology. This makes networks more scalable, resilient, and easier to manage, especially in large or complex environments. The role of dynamic routing becomes even more critical as organizations expand across multiple geographic locations, adopt cloud-based infrastructures, and implement redundant links for high availability.

At the heart of dynamic routing are the protocols that facilitate route advertisement and selection. These protocols enable routers to exchange information about the networks they can reach, evaluate multiple possible paths, and choose the best route based on specific metrics. Over time, as the network changes—whether due to link failures, topology updates, or newly added devices—dynamic routing protocols ensure that routing tables are automatically updated to reflect the most efficient and accurate path to each destination. This automatic adjustment process is a key benefit, as it reduces the administrative burden and helps maintain consistent connectivity throughout the network.

There are several families of dynamic routing protocols, each designed with specific goals and use cases in mind. The most commonly used protocols include OSPF (Open Shortest Path First), EIGRP (Enhanced Interior Gateway Routing Protocol), and BGP (Border Gateway Protocol). Each of these protocols has unique characteristics and operational mechanisms that make it suitable for particular networking scenarios. OSPF is a link-state protocol known for its fast convergence and hierarchical area design. It is widely used within enterprise and service provider networks. EIGRP, developed by Cisco, is a hybrid protocol that combines the features of distance-vector and link-state protocols, offering rapid convergence and scalability. BGP, in contrast, is the de facto standard for routing between autonomous systems on the internet. It is a path-vector protocol that prioritizes policy control and scalability over rapid convergence.

Dynamic routing is also deeply influenced by the concept of administrative distance, which is used by routers to determine the trustworthiness of a particular route source. When multiple routing protocols are in use, the router chooses the route with the lowest administrative distance to a given destination. This mechanism ensures that routers can intelligently prefer one protocol over another in environments where multiple protocols coexist. For example, a route learned via OSPF may be preferred over a route learned via RIP, depending on their respective administrative distances.

The evolution of networking hardware and software has led to widespread support for dynamic routing protocols across a variety of platforms. Cisco, Juniper, and MikroTik are three of the most prominent vendors that provide robust support for dynamic routing in their devices. Cisco's IOS, Juniper's Junos OS, and MikroTik's RouterOS each offer different configuration syntaxes and capabilities, but the underlying routing principles remain consistent. This cross-vendor support allows network engineers to design interoperable and redundant network infrastructures, even when different brands of equipment are used.

One of the most compelling aspects of dynamic routing is its ability to respond to failure and change. In a static routing environment, if a link goes down, traffic may be black-holed or rerouted inefficiently unless the administrator manually updates the configuration. Dynamic routing protocols detect failures using timers and hello messages, and can quickly reroute traffic through alternate paths. This level of adaptability is vital for maintaining service availability and minimizing downtime. In mission-critical environments, such as financial institutions, healthcare systems, and large-scale enterprise networks, even a few seconds of downtime can result in significant financial losses or operational disruptions. Therefore, dynamic routing not only improves efficiency but also contributes to business continuity.

Dynamic routing protocols use various metrics to determine the best path to a destination. These metrics may include bandwidth, delay, hop count, load, and reliability. Each protocol evaluates these metrics differently. OSPF, for example, calculates cost based primarily on bandwidth, while EIGRP uses a composite metric that includes bandwidth and delay. BGP, on the other hand, relies heavily on attributes such as AS-path length, local preference, and multi-exit discriminator to make routing decisions. Understanding how these metrics work is crucial for network engineers who want to influence routing behavior and optimize performance.

While dynamic routing simplifies many aspects of network management, it also introduces complexity and requires careful planning. Protocol selection, area and domain design, route summarization, and policy control are all critical components of a successful dynamic routing strategy. Poorly implemented dynamic routing can lead to routing loops, convergence issues, or even security vulnerabilities. For example, a misconfigured BGP peer could inadvertently propagate incorrect routing information, leading to widespread outages. Therefore, a deep understanding of protocol behavior, configuration best practices, and vendor-specific implementations is essential for building reliable and secure networks.

Dynamic routing is not limited to enterprise environments. It plays a crucial role in the functioning of the global internet. BGP, in particular, is responsible for connecting thousands of autonomous systems worldwide, each of which may represent an internet service provider, a data center, or a large organization. The dynamic exchange of routes between these systems allows internet traffic to find its way across continents, through undersea cables, and into remote regions. Without dynamic routing, the internet as we know it would not be able to function or scale to meet the demands of billions of users and devices.

In summary, dynamic routing is a cornerstone of modern network design and operation. It offers the flexibility, scalability, and resilience that today's networks require. Whether managing a small office network, a sprawling enterprise infrastructure, or a global data exchange, understanding dynamic routing is essential for any network professional. The protocols, behaviors, and configurations involved in dynamic routing form the basis for more advanced networking concepts and are crucial for certification paths such as Cisco's CCNA and CCNP, Juniper's JNCIA and JNCIP, and MikroTik's MTCNA and MTCRE. As networks continue to evolve with new technologies and demands, the importance of dynamic routing will only grow.

Chapter 2: Routing Protocol Fundamentals

Routing protocols are the mechanisms by which routers communicate with each other to share information about network topology and reachability. These protocols form the backbone of dynamic routing, enabling routers to exchange data, determine the most efficient paths for packet delivery, and adapt to changes in the network without manual intervention. Understanding the fundamental concepts of routing protocols is critical for any network engineer or IT professional working with IP networks, whether in small business environments or large-scale enterprise systems. At their core, routing protocols are designed to ensure that data can traverse complex networks efficiently, reliably, and securely.

Every router in a network has a routing table that it uses to determine where to send packets. These tables can be built statically, with routes manually defined by an administrator, or dynamically, with routes learned through routing protocols. The primary advantage of using dynamic routing protocols is their ability to respond to network changes in real time. When a link goes down or a new path becomes available, dynamic protocols update the routing tables automatically, often within seconds. This dynamic behavior makes them essential for networks that require high availability and quick failover capabilities.

Routing protocols fall into two main categories: interior gateway protocols (IGPs) and exterior gateway protocols (EGPs). IGPs operate within a single autonomous system—a network under a common administrative domain—while EGPs are used to exchange routing information between different autonomous systems. The most commonly used IGPs include OSPF (Open Shortest Path First), EIGRP (Enhanced Interior Gateway Routing Protocol), and RIP (Routing Information Protocol). On the other hand, BGP (Border Gateway Protocol) is the predominant EGP and is responsible for routing data across the global internet.

Each routing protocol uses a specific algorithm to determine the best path for sending packets. These algorithms rely on various metrics, which are values used to evaluate and compare different routes. Metrics can include hop count, bandwidth, delay, load, and reliability, depending on the protocol in use. For example, RIP uses hop count as its sole metric, which makes it simple but limited in scalability. OSPF uses cost based on link bandwidth, allowing it to make more intelligent path decisions. EIGRP uses a composite metric that includes bandwidth and delay, making it more flexible and precise. BGP, however, does not use traditional metrics; instead, it relies on path attributes like AS-path length, origin, local preference, and multi-exit discriminator to determine the best route.

Another important concept in routing protocols is convergence. Convergence refers to the process of all routers within a network agreeing on the best paths to all destinations. The speed at which this happens is known as convergence time, and it plays a crucial role in network stability. Faster convergence ensures minimal packet loss and downtime during network changes. Different protocols have varying convergence speeds. OSPF and EIGRP are known for their relatively fast convergence, while RIP is significantly slower. BGP, due to its complexity and the vast scope of the internet, converges more slowly and is often fine-tuned to prioritize stability over speed.

Routing protocols can also be categorized by how they share information. Distance-vector protocols, such as RIP and EIGRP, periodically share their entire routing table with their neighbors, relying on the distance to a destination as the main decision factor. In contrast, link-state protocols like OSPF build a complete map of the network by exchanging link-state advertisements (LSAs) and then independently calculating the shortest path using algorithms like Dijkstra's algorithm. This approach offers better scalability and more efficient use of bandwidth since updates are sent only when changes occur.

Loop prevention is another essential function of routing protocols. Routing loops occur when packets circulate endlessly in a network due to incorrect or outdated routing information. Each protocol employs different strategies to prevent such loops. RIP uses a maximum hop count of 15 to avoid routing loops, discarding any route that exceeds this number. EIGRP uses a technique called Diffusing Update Algorithm (DUAL), which ensures loop-free paths before a route is inserted into the routing table. OSPF uses a link-state database to ensure accurate and loop-free route calculations. BGP avoids loops by inspecting the AS-path attribute, rejecting routes that contain its own autonomous system number.

Administrative distance is another crucial element that routers use to choose between routes learned from different protocols. If a router receives the same route from OSPF and EIGRP, it will select the route with the lower administrative distance. For instance, EIGRP has an administrative distance of 90 for internal routes, while OSPF has a distance of 110. Therefore, the router will prefer the EIGRP-learned route unless manually configured otherwise. Understanding administrative distance is important when designing networks that utilize multiple routing protocols simultaneously, as it ensures predictable and consistent routing decisions.

Scalability and manageability are also key factors when selecting a routing protocol. Smaller networks may function adequately with RIP or static routing, but as the number of devices and subnets increases, more sophisticated protocols like OSPF, EIGRP, or BGP become necessary. These protocols support route summarization, hierarchical design, and advanced filtering techniques, which help reduce routing table size, improve performance, and enhance control over routing behavior.

Security in routing protocols is another area of increasing concern. Many protocols support authentication to prevent unauthorized devices from injecting false routing updates. OSPF supports MD5 and SHA authentication, while EIGRP and BGP also support various methods to verify the identity of peers. Without authentication, a malicious or misconfigured device could disrupt network operations by advertising incorrect routes. As networks become more exposed to external threats, securing the routing infrastructure becomes a top priority.

Finally, vendor implementations of routing protocols can differ in syntax and capabilities, but the core behaviors remain consistent. Cisco, Juniper, and MikroTik each provide tools and configuration models to implement dynamic routing. Understanding the underlying principles allows engineers to work across platforms and design interoperable networks. For example, even though Cisco IOS and Juniper Junos use different command-line interfaces, the configuration of OSPF or BGP follows the same logic: define the protocol, establish neighbor relationships, set up authentication if needed, and control route advertisement and filtering.

A solid grasp of routing protocol fundamentals is essential for building reliable, scalable, and secure networks. These protocols are the silent engines behind every packet that traverses the internet or an internal enterprise network. By mastering the mechanisms and logic behind routing protocols, network professionals gain the ability to troubleshoot complex issues, optimize performance, and design networks that adapt to change and growth with minimal disruption.

Chapter 3: Understanding Administrative Distance

Administrative distance is a fundamental concept in the world of dynamic routing that plays a crucial role in determining how routers choose between multiple paths to the same destination. When a router receives routing information from different sources—such as OSPF, EIGRP, RIP, or even static routes—it needs a method to determine which source is more trustworthy. This is where administrative distance comes into play. It is essentially a value that ranks the reliability of various routing protocols and route types. The lower the administrative distance, the more preferred the route. This metric ensures that routers make consistent and logical decisions when building their routing tables, especially in networks where multiple routing protocols coexist.

Every route that a router learns is associated with an administrative distance, which is pre-defined by default on most network devices, though it can also be manually adjusted by network engineers to suit specific design needs. For example, a directly connected interface has an administrative distance of 0, which makes it the most preferred. Static routes typically have a distance of 1, while EIGRP internal routes have a distance of 90 and OSPF routes have a default distance of 110. RIP, being one of the oldest and least sophisticated routing protocols, has a default administrative distance of 120. These values are critical for route selection, as a router will always install the route with the lowest administrative distance into its routing table when faced with multiple competing routes to the same destination.

Consider a scenario where a router learns about the same destination network from both EIGRP and OSPF. Without administrative distance, the router would have no clear method to choose between the two. But with EIGRP having a lower administrative distance than OSPF, the router will prefer the EIGRP-learned route and use it for packet forwarding. The OSPF-learned route remains in the routing database but is not installed in the active routing table unless the EIGRP route becomes unavailable. This fallback mechanism is one of the strengths of administrative distance, providing a simple and effective way to prioritize different sources of routing information.

Administrative distance is especially important in complex networks that use route redistribution. Redistribution occurs when routes learned by one routing protocol are injected into another. For example, a network might redistribute routes from OSPF into EIGRP and vice versa. This is often necessary when different parts of the network are running different protocols due to organizational policies, legacy systems, or vendor constraints. In such cases, careful manipulation of administrative distances is essential to avoid routing loops, suboptimal routing, or the unintentional selection of backup links over primary ones.

One of the key advantages of understanding administrative distance is the ability to influence route preference without having to alter the metrics of the routing protocols themselves. Metrics are protocol-specific and cannot be compared across protocols. For instance, OSPF uses cost, EIGRP uses a composite metric, and RIP uses hop count. These values are calculated differently and are not interoperable. Administrative distance provides a universal method to compare routes learned from different protocols. By adjusting administrative distances manually, network engineers can force a router to prefer one protocol over another for specific routes, even if the default metrics might suggest otherwise.

However, changing administrative distance must be done with caution. Lowering the distance of a less desirable route source can cause that route to override better, more stable routes. This can lead to performance degradation, increased latency, or even routing loops. It is critical to fully understand the implications of such changes, test them in a lab environment, and document them properly before deploying them in a production network. Improper use of administrative distance can lead to unpredictable network behavior and outages that are difficult to diagnose.

Administrative distance is also relevant in the context of static routing and floating static routes. A floating static route is a backup route configured with a higher administrative distance than a dynamic route. It remains inactive until the dynamic route fails. For example, a static route with an administrative distance of 200 can be used as a backup to an OSPF-learned route with a distance of 110. If the OSPF route disappears from the routing table due to a link failure or loss of adjacency, the router will activate the static route to maintain connectivity. This technique is commonly used for failover scenarios and provides a reliable method for ensuring high availability.

Another area where administrative distance plays a critical role is in multi-vendor environments. Different network devices may handle administrative distance slightly differently, especially when it comes to custom route types or redistributed routes. For instance, Cisco, Juniper, and MikroTik may use slightly different values for some non-standard protocols or assign different default distances to routes redistributed from connected, static, or default sources.

Understanding how each platform treats administrative distance is important when designing interoperable networks, especially when routes must be shared or redistributed across vendor boundaries.

In real-world enterprise environments, administrative distance serves not only as a technical tool but also as a strategic design element. It enables engineers to enforce routing policies, control traffic flow, and establish clear priorities between different route sources. When properly managed, it becomes a powerful mechanism to support route redundancy, load balancing, and policy-based routing decisions. Administrative distance can be fine-tuned to reflect organizational preferences, security considerations, and operational requirements, ensuring that the routing infrastructure aligns with broader IT and business goals.

The simplicity of administrative distance is deceptive, as it masks the complexity of the routing decisions that take place under the hood of every router. While it is just a numerical value, its influence on the path selection process is profound. It bridges the gap between disparate routing protocols and provides a standardized way to arbitrate between them. Every routing decision made by a router that has multiple route sources ultimately comes down to this small but powerful number. For network professionals, mastering administrative distance means gaining greater control over how data flows through the network, and having the confidence to build resilient, responsive, and intelligent routing architectures.

Chapter 4: OSPF Basics and Terminology

OSPF, or Open Shortest Path First, is one of the most widely used interior gateway routing protocols in enterprise networks. It is a link-state routing protocol, which means that it builds a complete map of the network topology by exchanging information about the state of each router's links with its neighbors. OSPF was designed to overcome the limitations of older distance-vector protocols like RIP, offering faster convergence, better scalability, support for large and complex networks, and more efficient use of network resources. Understanding OSPF begins with grasping its foundational concepts and terminology, which lay the groundwork for advanced configurations and design strategies.

At its core, OSPF operates by forming adjacencies between routers that are located within the same network segment. When two OSPF routers come online, they go through a process of neighbor discovery and adjacency formation using a series of message exchanges. These messages are called Hello packets, and they serve several purposes. Hello packets allow routers to discover each other, verify that communication is bidirectional, and ensure that both routers share the same configuration parameters such as area ID, hello and dead intervals, and authentication settings. If these parameters do not match, the routers will not form an adjacency.

Once adjacencies are formed, routers exchange information about their local topology through Link-State Advertisements, or LSAs. LSAs contain details about the router's interfaces, the networks it is connected to, the cost of those links, and any directly connected routers. All LSAs are stored in a database known as the Link-State Database, or LSDB. Each router builds and maintains its own LSDB, which is a synchronized map of the entire OSPF area's topology. Using this database, OSPF routers run Dijkstra's algorithm to calculate the shortest path to each destination network. The result of this calculation is the router's routing table, which is then used to forward packets.

OSPF is hierarchical by design, which is one of the reasons it scales so effectively. The concept of areas is central to this hierarchy. An OSPF area is a logical grouping of routers that share the same LSDB. All routers within an area have identical information about the area's topology, but they do not know the details of other areas. The core of an OSPF network is Area 0, also known as the backbone area. All other areas must connect directly to Area 0, either physically or through virtual links. This hierarchical structure reduces the size of each router's LSDB and limits the scope of LSA flooding, improving performance and simplifying troubleshooting.

There are several types of routers in OSPF, each serving a specific role in the network. Internal routers operate entirely within a single OSPF area and only have knowledge of that area's topology. Backbone routers are located within Area 0. Area Border Routers, or ABRs, connect one or more areas to the backbone and are responsible for summarizing and distributing routing information between areas. Autonomous System Boundary Routers, or ASBRs, connect the OSPF network to external routing domains such as BGP or another IGP. ASBRs import external routes into OSPF using Type 5 LSAs and make those routes available throughout the OSPF domain.

OSPF uses a cost metric to determine the best path to a destination. The cost is calculated based on the bandwidth of the link. By default, the cost is determined by dividing a reference bandwidth (typically 100 Mbps) by the interface bandwidth in Mbps. For example, a Fast Ethernet link with a bandwidth of 100 Mbps would have a cost of 1, while a 10 Mbps link would have a cost of 10. Lower costs are preferred, and the total cost of a path is the sum of the costs of all links along the path. Network administrators can manipulate OSPF costs to influence routing decisions and control traffic flow within the network.

LSAs are the building blocks of OSPF's link-state database and come in different types, each serving a unique purpose. Type 1 LSAs, also known as Router LSAs, describe the local interfaces of a router within an area. Type 2 LSAs are Network LSAs, used by designated routers on broadcast and non-broadcast multi-access networks to describe the routers connected to a common network segment. Type 3 LSAs, or Summary LSAs, are generated by ABRs to describe networks in other areas. Type 4 LSAs are used to inform routers in the OSPF domain about the presence of an ASBR. Type 5 LSAs carry information about external routes that are injected into OSPF from outside sources.

Designated Router (DR) and Backup Designated Router (BDR) roles are another important concept in OSPF, particularly on broadcast networks like Ethernet. To reduce the number of adjacencies and the amount of LSA flooding, OSPF elects a DR and a BDR on each multi-access segment. All other routers, called DROthers, form adjacencies only with the DR and BDR, not with each other. This election process is based on OSPF priority and router ID, with the highest value winning. The DR is responsible for generating Network LSAs and managing LSA distribution on the segment.

Router ID, or RID, is a unique identifier assigned to each OSPF router. It is a 32-bit number, usually represented in the format of an IP address. The router ID can be manually configured, or it can be automatically chosen based on the highest loopback interface IP address, or the highest active interface IP address if no loopbacks are configured. The router ID is used in all OSPF communications and remains fixed for the life of the OSPF process unless the process is restarted.

OSPF supports authentication to secure routing exchanges and prevent unauthorized routers from joining the OSPF domain. There are two main types of authentication: plain text and MD5 (or SHA in newer implementations). Authentication ensures that only trusted routers can participate in the OSPF network, protecting against malicious routing updates and misconfigurations that could lead to routing instability or security breaches.

Understanding the basics and terminology of OSPF provides a solid foundation for designing and operating robust and efficient networks. The protocol's link-state nature, hierarchical structure, and use of LSAs enable it to perform well in networks of all sizes. OSPF's support for scalability, fast convergence, and precise control over routing decisions makes it a preferred choice in enterprise environments and service provider infrastructures. As networks continue to grow and become more complex, the importance of mastering OSPF's principles and terminology will only increase.

Chapter 5: OSPF Packet Types

OSPF, or Open Shortest Path First, is a link-state routing protocol that relies on a series of specialized packet types to establish and maintain routing relationships between routers, exchange topology information, and ensure consistent network operation. These packet types are critical to the proper functioning of the protocol, and each serves a specific role within the OSPF process. OSPF is not just a protocol that passively receives information; it is an active protocol that continuously communicates with its peers using these packet types to ensure that the entire network has a synchronized view of the routing environment.

There are five main OSPF packet types, and each plays a role in a different phase of the OSPF process: Hello, Database Description (DBD), Link-State Request (LSR), Link-State Update (LSU), and Link-State Acknowledgment (LSAck). These packet types are used in a structured sequence as routers discover each other, form adjacencies, and exchange link-state information. The efficient use of these packets allows OSPF to converge quickly and maintain accurate routing tables even in complex and constantly changing network environments.

The Hello packet is the first type of packet used in OSPF, and it serves as the foundation for neighbor discovery and adjacency formation. When an OSPF-enabled interface comes up, it begins sending Hello packets at regular intervals. These packets are used to identify other OSPF routers on the same network segment. Hello packets include information such as the router's ID, the area ID, hello and dead intervals, the interface's priority, the list of known neighbors, and optional authentication data. Routers that receive a Hello packet will check this information to determine whether they can form an adjacency with the sender. If the parameters match and the router sees its own ID listed in the neighbor field, a bidirectional relationship is established. This process is essential for OSPF to function properly because only routers with bidirectional communication can become fully adjacent and participate in the exchange of routing information.

Once neighbors have been discovered and adjacencies are being formed, routers move to the next phase, which involves exchanging database summaries. This is where the Database Description packet comes into play. The DBD packet contains a summary of the LSAs in the sender's link-state database, including the type, ID, and sequence number of each LSA. The purpose of this exchange is to determine which LSAs the neighboring router already knows about and which ones it does not. By comparing DBD packets, routers can identify missing or outdated LSAs and request the ones they need using the next type of packet. The DBD process ensures that routers are synchronized in terms of their understanding of the network topology before proceeding with detailed updates.

After comparing DBD packets, a router may find that it needs more information about specific LSAs that it does not have or that are outdated. To retrieve this information, it sends a Link-State Request packet. LSR packets list the LSAs that the router is requesting from its neighbor. The LSR packet includes the LSA type, link-state ID, and advertising router ID for each requested LSA. This targeted request ensures that only necessary information is exchanged, reducing unnecessary traffic and making the synchronization process more efficient. The use of LSR packets helps maintain consistency between routers without overwhelming the network with redundant data.

In response to an LSR packet, a router sends the fourth type of OSPF packet: the Link-State Update. LSU packets contain one or more LSAs that have been requested or that need to be advertised. These LSAs provide detailed information about network links, such as router interfaces, network types, costs, and connected neighbors. An LSU can carry multiple LSAs in a single packet, making it efficient for distributing routing information. When a router receives an LSU, it updates its link-state database with the new information, provided that the LSA is more recent than what it currently has. The LSU is perhaps the most critical packet type in OSPF because it is responsible for actually distributing the link-state information that routers use to calculate the shortest path tree and populate the routing table.

To ensure reliability and prevent the loss of critical routing information, OSPF uses the fifth packet type: the Link-State Acknowledgment. When a router receives an LSU, it sends an LSAck packet to confirm receipt. This acknowledgment can be sent individually or can be grouped together for multiple LSAs. If a router does not receive an acknowledgment within a certain time period, it will retransmit the LSU to ensure that the data reaches its destination. This acknowledgment mechanism adds a layer of reliability to OSPF, ensuring that routing information is properly received and that the link-state databases remain synchronized across the network.

These five packet types work together in a highly organized and efficient manner. They allow OSPF routers to dynamically discover each other, establish reliable communication, exchange detailed routing information, and maintain up-to-date knowledge of the network topology. Unlike older protocols that rely on periodic full-table updates, OSPF minimizes bandwidth usage by only sending updates when changes occur and by sending only the specific pieces of information that are needed. This behavior makes OSPF particularly well-suited for large, complex, and hierarchical networks where efficiency and scalability are essential.

Each OSPF packet includes a standard header with key information such as the OSPF version, packet type, router ID, area ID, checksum, and authentication data. This header ensures that the packets can be properly validated and processed by receiving routers. The use of a standardized structure allows OSPF to function consistently across different vendors and implementations. Whether on Cisco, Juniper, or MikroTik devices, the behavior of these packet types remains the same, allowing for interoperability in multi-vendor environments.

Understanding OSPF packet types is essential for anyone looking to design, implement, or troubleshoot OSPF-based networks. Each packet type represents a specific stage in the OSPF process, and knowing how these packets interact provides insight into how the protocol maintains its link-state database and keeps the network operating smoothly. Misconfigurations, such as mismatched hello timers or incorrect area IDs, can be quickly diagnosed by examining packet exchanges and identifying where in the process the failure occurs. Network engineers who are familiar with the function and structure of OSPF packets are better equipped to optimize network performance, ensure fast convergence, and maintain a high level of availability in even the most demanding environments.

Chapter 6: OSPF Areas and Hierarchical Design

OSPF, or Open Shortest Path First, is a powerful and efficient link-state routing protocol designed to operate within large and complex networks. One of its most important architectural strengths is its ability to divide a network into multiple areas, allowing for a hierarchical design that enhances scalability, reduces routing overhead, and improves manageability. The concept of areas in OSPF is fundamental, as it introduces a logical segmentation of the network that controls the spread of routing information and minimizes unnecessary processing on routers that do not need to know about every detail of the network topology.

An OSPF area is a group of routers that share the same link-state database and have a consistent view of the topology within that specific portion of the network. By breaking up a network into different areas, OSPF helps limit the scope of link-state advertisements and reduces the size of each router's database, which in turn lowers memory usage and CPU load. This is especially important in networks that continue to grow in size and complexity, where having a single flat topology would overwhelm routers and slow down convergence times. Each OSPF area is identified by a unique Area ID, which is commonly represented in dotted decimal format, such as 0.0.0.1, although it can also be expressed as a simple decimal number.

At the core of every OSPF network is Area 0, also known as the backbone area. This area plays a central role in the hierarchical design of OSPF, as all other areas must connect to it either directly or through a virtual link. The backbone area is responsible for transporting routing information between non-backbone areas, making it the central hub for inter-area communication. If an area is not connected to Area 0, OSPF will not be able to propagate routing information between it and other areas. This requirement ensures a clear and predictable path for routing updates and helps maintain the protocol's internal structure.

Routers within an OSPF network can serve different roles depending on their location and function. Internal routers are those whose interfaces are all within the same area. These routers only maintain a single link-state database for that area and do not participate in inter-area routing. Area Border Routers, or ABRs, are connected to multiple areas, including Area 0 and at least one non-backbone area. ABRs maintain separate link-state databases for each area they are connected to and are responsible for summarizing and distributing routing information between areas. They are critical components in the OSPF hierarchy, as they control the flow of information across the entire OSPF domain.

Another type of router, the Autonomous System Boundary Router, or ASBR, sits at the edge of the OSPF domain and exchanges routing information with external networks, such as those running different routing protocols like BGP or RIP. The ASBR injects external routes into OSPF using Type 5 or Type 7 LSAs, depending on the area type. These external routes are then advertised throughout the OSPF network, allowing internal routers to reach destinations outside of the OSPF-controlled environment. ASBRs play an essential role in integrating OSPF with other routing domains and enabling enterprise networks to connect to the internet or partner networks.

The use of areas allows for more granular control of routing information. Within an area, routers share detailed topology information through link-state advertisements, which provide a full map of the area. However, routers in one area do not receive the same level of detail about other areas. Instead, they receive summarized information from ABRs. This summarization is one of the key benefits of OSPF's hierarchical design, as it reduces the volume of routing information that needs to be processed and exchanged. By summarizing routes at the area boundary, OSPF limits the impact of topology changes in one area on the rest of the network, improving stability and performance.

Several special area types in OSPF further enhance the protocol's flexibility. A stub area is designed to block external route advertisements, reducing the size of the routing table for routers within the area. Instead of receiving external routes, routers in a stub area rely on a default route provided by the ABR. This is useful in remote or branch locations where resources are limited and where full visibility of external routes is not necessary. A variation of the stub area is the totally stubby area, which not only blocks external routes but also suppresses inter-area routes, allowing only intra-area routes and a default route to be advertised. This further simplifies the routing table and minimizes processing requirements.

Another specialized area type is the Not-So-Stubby Area, or NSSA. This type of area allows the injection of external routes into the OSPF domain while still maintaining some of the benefits of a stub area. NSSAs use Type 7 LSAs to carry external route information, which is later converted to Type 5 LSAs by an ABR when it leaves the NSSA and enters the backbone. This configuration is particularly useful when an ASBR is located within an area that would otherwise be stubbed. It provides a balance between the need to limit routing information and the requirement to reach external destinations.

Virtual links are a mechanism in OSPF that allow an area that is not directly connected to Area 0 to be logically connected to it. This is necessary when network design constraints or legacy infrastructure prevent a physical connection to the backbone. Virtual links are established between two ABRs and tunnel OSPF traffic across intermediate areas to ensure backbone connectivity. While virtual links provide flexibility, they are generally considered a workaround and should be used sparingly, as they can introduce additional complexity and potential points of failure.

The design of OSPF areas must be approached thoughtfully, with consideration given to the size of each area, the number of routers, and the expected level of routing activity. Best practices recommend limiting the number of routers per area to around 50, although this number can vary based on hardware capabilities and traffic patterns. Proper summarization, a well-planned area hierarchy, and clear separation of roles for ABRs and ASBRs all contribute to a stable and efficient OSPF deployment.

A hierarchical OSPF design not only improves network scalability but also enhances control over routing policies, simplifies troubleshooting, and enables better use of available bandwidth and resources. It provides a clear framework for organizing large networks into manageable segments, allowing engineers to optimize performance and minimize the impact of network changes. With its structured approach to routing and the flexibility of area design, OSPF continues to be one of the most effective and reliable protocols for enterprise and service provider networks alike.

Chapter 7: OSPF Neighbor Establishment

OSPF neighbor establishment is the first and one of the most critical steps in the operation of the OSPF routing protocol. Before routers can exchange link-state information and build a complete picture of the network topology, they must first discover one another, verify compatibility, and establish a relationship known as an OSPF adjacency. This process is methodical, structured, and follows a specific sequence of states that ensure the stability, synchronization, and reliability of routing information across the OSPF domain. Understanding how OSPF neighbors are formed provides insight into how OSPF operates at a fundamental level and is essential for configuring and troubleshooting OSPF networks effectively.

When an OSPF-enabled router interface becomes active, it begins sending Hello packets at regular intervals. These Hello packets are multicast messages that serve as the initial introduction between OSPF routers on the same network segment. The Hello packet contains important parameters that must match between routers for a neighbor relationship to be established. These parameters include the OSPF area ID, hello interval, dead interval, authentication type and key (if used), and stub area flag. If even one of these parameters does not match, the neighbor relationship will not form, and the routers will ignore each other's Hello packets. This strict matching process helps maintain consistency and ensures that routers with incompatible configurations do not exchange routing information.

When a router receives a Hello packet that matches all required parameters, it checks the neighbor list inside the packet to see if its own router ID is included. If it is, this indicates that bidirectional communication has been established. Bidirectional communication is a prerequisite for forming an adjacency. Once bidirectional communication is confirmed, the neighbor relationship progresses through a series of states designed to ensure that both routers are ready and able to exchange routing information safely and efficiently.

The first state in this sequence is the Down state, which means that no Hello packets have been received from the neighbor. This is the default state before any communication begins. Once a Hello packet is received, the router enters the Init state. In the Init state, the router recognizes the presence of another OSPF router but has not yet confirmed two-way communication. If the neighbor's Hello packet includes the router's own ID in the neighbor list, the router transitions to the Two-Way state. This state confirms that bidirectional communication exists, and it is also the final state for most routers on a broadcast network that do not become fully adjacent.

On broadcast and non-broadcast multi-access networks, OSPF uses a designated router (DR) and a backup designated router (BDR) to reduce the number of adjacencies and minimize the exchange of LSAs. In these environments, routers in the Two-Way state will not form full adjacencies with all neighbors, but only with the DR and BDR. The election of the DR and BDR is determined by OSPF priority and router ID. Once the DR and BDR are elected, the routers that will become fully adjacent transition to the ExStart state.

In the ExStart state, the two routers determine which one will start the exchange process by comparing their router IDs. The router with the higher ID becomes the master, while the other becomes the slave. This master-slave relationship controls the sequence of database description packets that follow. After the ExStart state, the routers move into the Exchange state, where they begin exchanging Database Description (DBD) packets. These packets contain summaries of each router's link-state database, including LSA headers with information about each advertised link. This allows routers to identify which LSAs they have in common and which ones need to be requested or updated.

Once DBD packets are exchanged and each router knows which LSAs it is missing or which are outdated, the routers enter the Loading state. In this state, routers send Link-State Request (LSR) packets to request the full details of specific LSAs they need. The neighboring router responds with Link-State Update (LSU) packets containing the requested LSAs. As these LSAs are received and processed, the routers continue to update their link-state databases and recalculate the shortest path tree using Dijkstra's algorithm. The reliability of the LSA exchange is ensured through the use of Link-State Acknowledgment (LSAck) packets, which confirm the successful receipt of each update.

Finally, when all necessary LSAs have been exchanged and both routers have fully synchronized their databases, the adjacency reaches the Full state. In the Full state, the routers are considered fully adjacent and can now participate in routing decisions and topology changes. If a change in the network occurs, such as a link going down or a new router joining, the routers that are in the Full state will immediately begin the process of flooding updated LSAs, recalculating routes, and maintaining a consistent view of the network topology.

The entire OSPF neighbor establishment process is designed with stability and scalability in mind. By forming full adjacencies only where necessary and using designated routers to manage LSA flooding, OSPF minimizes the amount of overhead traffic and reduces the processing load on each router. This design allows OSPF to perform well in both small networks and large, complex enterprise environments. The use of clear and predictable neighbor states also simplifies troubleshooting. For instance, if two routers are stuck in the Init or ExStart state, this usually indicates a configuration mismatch, MTU issue, or faulty interface. By analyzing the state transitions, network engineers can quickly pinpoint the source of the problem and implement a solution.

Understanding OSPF neighbor establishment is not just about memorizing states or recognizing packet types. It is about grasping the logical flow of communication between routers and appreciating the design choices that make OSPF a reliable and efficient protocol. The neighbor process is the first line of coordination in a distributed routing protocol, and it sets the tone for everything that follows. When routers are properly introduced and synchronized, the OSPF domain functions as a cohesive system, capable of adapting to change and maintaining consistent routing decisions across a diverse and dynamic network landscape.

Chapter 8: OSPF Metric and Cost Calculation

In OSPF, the metric used to determine the best path to a destination network is known as cost. Cost is a numerical value that represents the overhead required to send packets across a particular interface. Unlike some other routing protocols that use simple metrics such as hop count, OSPF uses a more sophisticated approach that takes into account the bandwidth of the link. The lower the cost, the more preferred the path. This allows OSPF to make intelligent routing decisions based on the actual capabilities of the network, rather than just the number of hops between routers.

The cost of an OSPF route is calculated based on the sum of the costs of all outgoing interfaces along the path to the destination. Each interface on a router is assigned a cost, which is derived from the bandwidth of the link. By default, OSPF uses the formula cost = reference bandwidth divided by interface bandwidth. The reference bandwidth is typically set to 100 Mbps in many OSPF implementations, though this value can and should be adjusted in modern networks where high-speed links of 1 Gbps, 10 Gbps, or even faster are common. If the reference bandwidth is not adjusted accordingly, all high-speed links may end up having the same cost, which can result in inefficient routing decisions.

For example, if a router has an interface with a bandwidth of 100 Mbps, and the reference bandwidth is set to 100 Mbps, the calculated cost for that interface would be 1. A slower link with a bandwidth of 10 Mbps would have a cost of 10. A faster link with 1 Gbps would have a cost of 0.1, but since OSPF only uses integer values for cost, it would also be interpreted as 1 unless the reference bandwidth is increased to better differentiate between link speeds. This illustrates the importance of carefully tuning the reference bandwidth in environments where multiple types of links coexist.

The reference bandwidth is a global setting on a router and should be consistent across the entire OSPF domain to avoid routing inconsistencies. In Cisco devices, for example, the reference bandwidth can be changed with a simple command, allowing network engineers to reflect the true value of modern high-speed links. Failing to update this setting can lead to situations where a high-capacity link is treated as equal to a much slower one, potentially leading to congestion and performance issues.

OSPF does not dynamically adjust cost based on real-time traffic, latency, or load. It assumes that the link bandwidth is a reliable indicator of performance. This is both a strength and a limitation. On one hand, it provides stability and predictability, since cost values do not fluctuate with traffic levels. On the other hand, it does not take into account other important factors like delay, jitter, or packet loss. However, this simplicity is one of the reasons OSPF converges quickly and remains relatively easy to configure and troubleshoot, even in large environments.

In multi-access networks, such as Ethernet, the cost assigned to the interface applies to traffic sent out through that interface regardless of the destination. In point-to-point links, the cost is more direct, and it reflects the characteristics of a single, dedicated path. This difference becomes especially important in network designs that use both types of links. In point-to-multipoint configurations, OSPF treats the network as a series of individual point-to-point links and calculates the cost separately for each peer. This can be particularly useful in scenarios involving Frame Relay or MPLS-based VPNs, where the logical topology may not match the physical layout.

Manual cost configuration is another tool that network engineers can use to influence OSPF path selection. In cases where two links have the same default cost, but one link is preferred due to security, reliability, or policy reasons, the administrator can manually set the interface cost to guide OSPF's decisions. This gives a high level of control over traffic engineering without the need to adjust physical bandwidth or rely on dynamic protocols. It also allows for redundancy planning by ensuring that backup paths have higher costs and are only used when primary links fail.

One of the key advantages of OSPF's cost-based metric is its additive nature. Since OSPF calculates the total cost to a destination as the sum of interface costs along the path, it is able to distinguish between multiple paths and always choose the one with the lowest cumulative cost. This is fundamentally different from distance-vector protocols like RIP, which consider only the number of hops and are blind to the quality or bandwidth of each link. As a result, OSPF provides more granular and accurate route selection, especially in networks with diverse link types and varying performance characteristics.

When a change occurs in the network, such as a link failure or a new route becoming available, OSPF recalculates the shortest path tree using Dijkstra's algorithm, also known as the SPF (Shortest Path First) algorithm. This calculation takes into account the cost of all possible paths to each destination and selects the one with the lowest total cost. The router then updates its routing table and begins forwarding traffic along the new best path. Because cost is the only metric used in OSPF, all routing decisions hinge on these values, making accurate cost assignment vital for maintaining optimal network performance.

Cost calculation in OSPF also plays a role in load balancing. If two or more paths to a destination have exactly the same cost, OSPF can install all of them into the routing table and perform equal-cost multi-path (ECMP) routing. This allows the router to balance traffic across multiple links, increasing bandwidth utilization and improving redundancy. ECMP is particularly beneficial in data center and service provider environments, where parallel links are common and maximizing throughput is essential. However, ECMP only works when the costs are identical, so careful planning and consistent configuration are required to enable this feature.

The concept of OSPF cost and metric calculation might seem straightforward at first, but its influence on the behavior of an OSPF network is profound. Every routing decision, every convergence event, and every failover scenario depends on how costs are configured and interpreted. Network engineers must therefore develop a strong understanding of how cost is calculated, how it can be influenced, and how it affects overall network design. By mastering this concept, they gain the ability to build OSPF networks that are not only efficient and reliable but also flexible enough to accommodate the unique needs of any environment.

Chapter 9: OSPF Network Types

OSPF is a highly flexible and intelligent routing protocol that can operate efficiently across a variety of network topologies. One of the reasons for this flexibility is its ability to adapt its behavior depending on the type of network to which an interface is connected. OSPF defines several distinct network types, and each one influences how OSPF routers form adjacencies, exchange routing information, elect designated routers, and flood link-state advertisements. Understanding these network types is essential for deploying OSPF in a way that maximizes efficiency, minimizes unnecessary overhead, and ensures consistent routing behavior across the network.

The most common and widely understood OSPF network type is the broadcast network. This type is typically associated with Ethernet segments where multiple routers can communicate with each other using multicast or broadcast messages. In a broadcast network, OSPF assumes that all routers on the segment can hear each other's Hello packets. To optimize performance and reduce the number of adjacencies formed, OSPF uses the concept of a designated router (DR) and a backup designated router (BDR). Rather than forming a full mesh of adjacencies between all routers on the segment, each router forms an adjacency only with the DR and BDR. The DR becomes responsible for generating and distributing Network LSAs on behalf of the segment, which describe the topology of that multi-access link. This dramatically reduces the number of LSAs and helps OSPF scale in large broadcast environments. The election of the DR and BDR is determined by OSPF priority and, in the event of a tie, the router ID.

Another important OSPF network type is the non-broadcast multi-access network, commonly abbreviated as NBMA. NBMA networks are similar to broadcast networks in that they can have multiple routers connected to a common network segment, but they do not support broadcast or multicast communication. Examples of NBMA networks include Frame Relay, X.25, and certain MPLS-based VPN configurations. In NBMA environments, OSPF cannot rely on multicast Hello packets to discover neighbors automatically, so neighbors must be manually defined. Static neighbor configuration is required to ensure that routers can communicate and form adjacencies. OSPF still uses the DR and BDR model on NBMA networks, but without automatic discovery, the DR and BDR must also be manually configured or determined during the adjacency process. This makes NBMA networks more administratively intensive and prone to misconfiguration if not carefully managed.

Point-to-point networks are another OSPF network type and are generally the simplest and most straightforward to configure. These are typically links where only two routers are connected directly, such as serial connections or Ethernet interfaces in routed point-to-point mode. In this type of network, OSPF assumes that there is only one other router on the link, and therefore there is no need for a DR or BDR. Each router simply forms a full adjacency with the other and exchanges LSAs directly. The simplicity of point-to-point networks makes them ideal for backbone connections, site-to-site WAN links, and other scenarios where clear, dedicated communication paths exist between routers. OSPF's behavior on point-to-point links results in faster convergence and fewer resources spent managing unnecessary roles or adjacencies.

Another variation is the point-to-multipoint network type. This type is used in topologies where a single interface on a router is connected to multiple endpoints, but those endpoints are treated as individual point-to-point connections. This is often used in environments like Frame Relay or DMVPN, where multiple remote sites connect to a central hub over virtual circuits. In point-to-multipoint mode, OSPF does not elect a DR or BDR, and each remote site forms a full adjacency with the central router. Link-state advertisements describe each connection individually, providing greater visibility and control. This model eliminates the need for static neighbor definitions, which are required in NBMA networks, and provides more accurate metric calculation, as each link is treated independently. While point-to-multipoint networks may generate more LSAs than NBMA or broadcast networks, the trade-off is simplified configuration and more reliable operation in hub-and-spoke environments.

There is also the point-to-multipoint non-broadcast network type. This is similar to point-to-multipoint, but it operates in an environment where broadcast and multicast communication is not supported. In this case, routers must manually define their neighbors, as OSPF cannot use Hello multicasts to automatically discover them. This type allows greater flexibility in non-broadcast environments while preserving the simplified topology of a point-to-multipoint design. However, because it combines the administrative burden of NBMA networks with the LSA behavior of point-to-multipoint networks, it is generally used only when required by the limitations of the physical network infrastructure.

Each OSPF network type influences how Hello packets are sent and received, how adjacencies are formed, and how LSAs are generated and flooded. For example, on a broadcast network, Hello packets are multicast to the AllSPFRouters address, and adjacencies are limited to the DR and BDR. On a point-to-point link, Hello packets are also multicast, but only one adjacency is formed, and there is no DR or BDR. On an NBMA network, Hello packets must be unicast to each neighbor, and all neighbors must be manually defined. These operational differences affect everything from convergence time to troubleshooting and should always be considered when designing an OSPF topology.

Choosing the correct network type is essential for optimal OSPF performance and stability. In many cases, the network type is automatically assigned based on the interface type, but network administrators can manually override it to better match the network's physical or logical characteristics. Misconfigured network types can lead to routing problems, failed adjacencies, and inefficient LSA flooding. For instance, configuring a broadcast interface as point-to-point will disable DR election and may lead to incomplete adjacencies. Conversely, misclassifying a point-to-point link as a broadcast network may result in unnecessary DR elections and confusion in the LSA database.

The OSPF network type also affects troubleshooting methodologies. When adjacency issues occur, understanding the expected behavior for the network type helps isolate the problem. On broadcast networks, a failure to elect a DR may prevent routers from reaching the Full state. On NBMA networks, missing neighbor statements may prevent adjacency altogether. On point-to-multipoint links, incorrect configurations can result in incomplete LSA generation or improper metric calculation. The ability to recognize and respond to these issues begins with a solid understanding of how OSPF behaves in each type of network environment.

The flexibility of OSPF to support multiple network types reflects its maturity and robustness as a dynamic routing protocol. It can adapt to a wide range of physical and logical topologies while maintaining reliable routing behavior and fast convergence. By leveraging the right network type for each segment, network engineers can ensure that OSPF operates efficiently, minimizes overhead, and delivers consistent performance across the enterprise. The ability to design OSPF networks with the appropriate network types is a key skill that distinguishes effective network architects and plays a vital role in building scalable and resilient IP infrastructures.

Chapter 10: OSPF Authentication Methods

OSPF, being a routing protocol that operates by exchanging information between routers, must ensure that the data it receives and processes is legitimate. In dynamic routing, unauthorized or malicious updates can compromise the integrity of the routing table and lead to severe consequences such as routing loops, black holes, traffic interception, or full denial of service. To prevent these types of security threats, OSPF provides built-in authentication mechanisms that allow routers to verify the identity of their neighbors and ensure that the routing information exchanged is trustworthy. These authentication methods are an essential component of a secure OSPF deployment, especially in environments where multiple devices are interconnected across public or semi-trusted networks.

There are three primary authentication methods supported by OSPF: no authentication, plain-text authentication, and cryptographic authentication. These methods are defined per OSPF area or per interface, and they govern how OSPF packets are validated when received by a router. The default method is no authentication, meaning that routers trust all incoming OSPF packets from interfaces in that area or network segment. While this may be acceptable in isolated or highly controlled environments, it is not suitable for production networks where potential threats can originate from misconfigured or compromised devices. Without authentication, any router that is configured to speak OSPF and has access to the network could potentially influence routing decisions simply by sending forged LSAs.

Plain-text authentication provides a basic level of security by including a clear-text password in each OSPF packet. This password is configured on all routers within the same area or network segment. When a router receives an OSPF packet, it checks the authentication field and compares the password to its local configuration. If the passwords match, the packet is accepted; otherwise, it is discarded. This mechanism ensures that only routers with the correct shared password can participate in OSPF. However, because the password is transmitted in clear text, it can be intercepted and read by anyone with access to the network traffic. This method offers minimal protection and should be considered only for low-risk or temporary environments.

For stronger security, OSPF supports cryptographic authentication, commonly implemented using MD5 or HMAC-SHA algorithms, depending on the router platform and OSPF version. In cryptographic authentication, the password is not sent over the network. Instead, a cryptographic hash is generated using the packet contents and the configured key. The hash is appended to the packet in the authentication field. When a neighboring router receives the packet, it uses the same key to generate its own hash and compares it to the received one. If the hashes match, the packet is accepted as authentic. This method prevents unauthorized devices from forging valid OSPF packets unless they possess the correct key.

MD5 authentication is the most widely used cryptographic method in traditional OSPF environments. It is supported across Cisco, Juniper, MikroTik, and other vendor platforms. To implement MD5 authentication, a key is configured with an identifier and an associated hash value. All routers on the same OSPF segment must use the same key ID and key value for authentication to succeed. When properly implemented, MD5 authentication ensures the integrity and authenticity of OSPF routing exchanges. While MD5 is no longer considered cryptographically secure against determined attackers due to known vulnerabilities, it still provides a much higher level of security than plain-text passwords and is commonly used in enterprise networks where stronger options are not available.

Newer implementations of OSPF, particularly those aligned with OSPFv3 and IPv6, support stronger authentication mechanisms based on IPsec and HMAC-SHA algorithms. Unlike OSPFv2, which includes authentication fields within the OSPF packet itself, OSPFv3 relies on the IP layer for authentication and encryption, separating routing and security functions. This allows OSPFv3 to use the full capabilities of modern security protocols, including mutual authentication, replay protection, and encryption of routing messages. HMAC-SHA1 and HMAC-SHA256 are commonly used algorithms in this context, offering significantly better security than MD5.

When deploying OSPF authentication, consistency across routers is critical. All routers on a common network segment or within the same area must use the same authentication method and configuration, or they will fail to establish adjacencies. Authentication mismatches can result in routers remaining in the Init or ExStart state, unable to complete the neighbor relationship. This can lead to incomplete routing tables and communication failures across the network. Therefore, careful planning and documentation are essential when configuring OSPF authentication, especially in large or multi-vendor environments where syntax and capabilities may vary.

Key management is another important aspect of OSPF authentication. To maintain security over time, it is necessary to change authentication keys periodically. Many router platforms support key rotation using key chains, which allow multiple keys to be defined with different lifetimes. The router can automatically switch keys based on time or administrative command, minimizing disruption while maintaining secure communication. This feature is particularly valuable in environments with strict security compliance requirements, where frequent key changes are mandated by policy.

Troubleshooting OSPF authentication issues requires a solid understanding of the packet exchange process and the tools available on the router. Administrators can use commands to inspect OSPF neighbor states, view authentication settings, and monitor for rejected packets. On Cisco routers, for example, commands like show ip ospf interface and debug ip ospf adj reveal valuable information about whether authentication is enabled, what key is being used, and why a particular neighbor relationship is failing. On Juniper devices, similar insights can be obtained through operational mode commands and log files. Observing log messages and packet captures can quickly reveal if there is a password mismatch, a timing issue, or a hash calculation failure.

OSPF authentication not only protects the integrity of routing information but also contributes to the overall security posture of a network. As routing protocols form the foundation of communication between devices, securing these exchanges is vital to ensuring the confidentiality, availability, and reliability of the entire infrastructure. With the increasing sophistication of network attacks and the growing interconnection of systems, neglecting authentication in dynamic routing protocols is no longer acceptable. While OSPF was originally designed for trusted environments, its evolution to include strong authentication methods reflects the need to operate safely in modern, heterogeneous, and sometimes hostile network conditions.

Implementing OSPF authentication is not merely a technical task but a strategic decision that aligns network operations with organizational security policies. Whether securing a simple branch-to-branch OSPF link or deploying cryptographic authentication across a multi-area enterprise topology, the principles remain the same: validate every neighbor, protect every route, and ensure that only trusted devices can influence the path that data takes through the network. When used effectively, OSPF authentication provides a crucial layer of defense against misconfiguration, human error, and malicious interference in the most critical component of any network infrastructure.

Chapter 11: OSPF Route Summarization

OSPF is a link-state routing protocol known for its scalability and efficiency in large and complex networks. One of the key techniques that supports this scalability is route summarization. Route summarization, also known as route aggregation, is the process of combining several contiguous subnets into a single summary route. In OSPF, this technique is used to reduce the size of routing tables, limit the scope of topology changes, and enhance the overall performance and stability of the routing domain. Although OSPF does not perform automatic summarization like some distance-vector protocols such as EIGRP, it supports manual summarization at specific points in the network, and when implemented correctly, it brings significant operational benefits.

In OSPF, route summarization is only possible at two key locations: on Area Border Routers (ABRs) and on Autonomous System Boundary Routers (ASBRs). ABRs are responsible for summarizing routes between areas, while ASBRs summarize external routes being redistributed into the OSPF domain from other routing protocols or static configurations. Within a single OSPF area, there is no route summarization because all routers in that area must maintain a synchronized and detailed view of the network topology. This is due to the link-state nature of OSPF, where routers rely on identical link-state databases to build accurate and loop-free routing tables using Dijkstra's algorithm.

Route summarization on an ABR allows the router to advertise a single summary route that represents multiple subnets located in a connected area. For example, if Area 1 contains several subnets such as 10.1.1.0/24, 10.1.2.0/24, and 10.1.3.0/24, the ABR can be configured to summarize these into a single route such as 10.1.0.0/22 when advertising them into Area 0. This process reduces the number of entries in the routing table for routers in other areas, which not only conserves memory and CPU resources but also improves convergence time when network changes occur. Without summarization, each of those subnets would be advertised individually, leading to a larger and potentially more volatile routing table.

ASBRs, which redistribute external routes from other routing protocols into OSPF, also benefit from summarization. When large numbers of external routes are introduced into an OSPF domain, they are flooded throughout all areas by default as Type 5 LSAs. This can significantly increase the size of the link-state database and the computational burden on routers. By summarizing these routes at the point of redistribution, the ASBR reduces the number of LSAs that must be processed and stored by OSPF routers. For example, if an ASBR is redistributing a range of static routes such as 192.168.1.0/24 through 192.168.14.0/24, it can summarize them into 192.168.0.0/20, assuming the addressing allows for it. This not only simplifies the LSA database but also shields the OSPF domain from unnecessary detail.

Route summarization also plays an important role in improving network stability. When a specific subnet within a summarized range experiences a failure, routers outside of the summarizing area do not need to recompute their SPF trees, as the summary route remains valid. Only the routers within the originating area or domain need to adjust their link-state databases. This isolation of topology changes reduces the scope of LSA flooding and recalculation, resulting in faster convergence and fewer disruptions in the wider network. Summarization thus acts as a boundary that contains the effects of localized issues, which is particularly valuable in large-scale deployments.

Careful planning is required when implementing route summarization in OSPF. Summarizing routes incorrectly can lead to routing black holes, where traffic is sent toward a summary route that no longer leads to any valid destination. This can happen if all the specific subnets covered by the summary become unreachable but the summary is still advertised. Routers that receive the summary continue forwarding traffic based on outdated information, causing packets to be dropped. To mitigate this risk, some implementations allow for conditional advertisement of summary routes based on reachability of the included subnets. However, not all platforms support this feature, and administrators must ensure that at least one subnet within the summary remains available or implement additional safeguards using route filtering and policy routing.

Another consideration in route summarization is the alignment of IP addressing schemes. Summarization is only possible when subnets are contiguous and can be represented as a single block using a common prefix. If subnets are scattered or irregularly assigned, summarization becomes inefficient or impossible. For this reason, IP address planning is essential in networks that intend to leverage summarization. Assigning address blocks in a structured and hierarchical manner allows for more effective summaries and supports future growth and reorganization without compromising routing efficiency.

On Cisco routers, OSPF route summarization is configured differently depending on whether it is being done on an ABR or an ASBR. For ABRs, the area range command is used under the OSPF process configuration. For ASBRs, the summary-address command is used under the redistribution configuration. Other vendors, such as Juniper and MikroTik, provide similar mechanisms with different syntaxes but follow the same principles. Understanding the behavior and configuration methods of each platform is critical for implementing summarization correctly and consistently in multi-vendor environments.

Route summarization also affects how default routes are propagated in OSPF. A common design pattern involves injecting a default route into an area as a summary to represent all external or unknown destinations. For example, an ABR can advertise 0.0.0.0/0 into a stub or totally stubby area to direct all non-local traffic toward a centralized exit point. This practice simplifies routing tables for routers in remote areas and avoids the need to advertise every possible external destination individually. In larger enterprise or service provider networks, summarizing routes at the edge or redistribution points helps maintain clean and manageable routing domains that are easier to troubleshoot and optimize.

Ultimately, route summarization is a powerful tool in OSPF that contributes to efficient network design and operation. It minimizes unnecessary detail in routing updates, improves the performance of the OSPF protocol, and provides better control over how routing information is disseminated across the network. By reducing the number of LSAs and limiting the scope of changes, it helps maintain fast and stable convergence. When applied correctly and supported by thoughtful IP addressing and router configuration, OSPF summarization enables scalable and resilient networks that can handle growth, change, and complexity with confidence.

Chapter 12: OSPF Stub and NSSA Areas

OSPF, by design, allows for a hierarchical structure through the use of areas, and this structure plays a vital role in enabling scalability and efficiency in large networks. One of the key benefits of using multiple areas is the ability to control and limit the propagation of routing information. Within this architecture, OSPF introduces special types of areas known as stub areas and Not-So-Stubby Areas (NSSAs), both of which are designed to reduce the amount of routing information exchanged and stored in the OSPF database. These area types serve to simplify routing for routers in less critical parts of the network, often in branch or remote office locations, where full routing knowledge is unnecessary or inefficient.

A stub area is a type of OSPF area that does not accept external routes, specifically Type 5 LSAs, which are used to advertise networks from outside the OSPF autonomous system. These external routes may come from redistribution of other routing protocols like BGP or static routes into OSPF. In a stub area, these Type 5 LSAs are filtered out by the Area Border Router, and instead, the ABR injects a single default route (0.0.0.0/0) into the area. This default route acts as a catch-all for destinations not explicitly known within the area, allowing routers inside the stub to reach external networks without needing full details about them. This simplification reduces the number of entries in the routing table and minimizes the size of the link-state database, which improves performance, especially for routers with limited resources.

Stub areas are particularly beneficial in hub-and-spoke topologies where multiple branch offices connect to a central site. The branches typically do not need to know the details of the entire network, as they will send most non-local traffic to the central site anyway. By configuring these remote branches as stub areas, administrators reduce the load on branch routers and improve the overall stability of the OSPF domain. However, all routers within a stub area must agree on its type; they must be configured as stub in order to form adjacencies and exchange routing information properly. A mismatch in stub configuration results in adjacency failures, and the OSPF routers will remain stuck in the Init or ExStart state.

Another variant of the stub area is the totally stubby area, a term commonly associated with Cisco implementations. In a totally stubby area, not only are Type 5 LSAs blocked, but also inter-area routes represented by Type 3 LSAs are suppressed. This means that routers inside a totally stubby area only receive a default route from the ABR and do not learn about networks in other areas. This approach further reduces routing complexity and is ideal for sites that should send all traffic, both external and inter-area, through a single exit point. While this model greatly simplifies routing tables, it also removes the possibility of more granular routing decisions, which may not be suitable for all scenarios.

Despite the benefits of stub and totally stubby areas, there are situations where external routes must be injected into an OSPF area, even if the area is meant to be lightweight. This is where Not-So-Stubby Areas, or NSSAs, come into play. An NSSA is a hybrid OSPF area type that allows for limited external route injection while still blocking traditional Type 5 LSAs. Instead of propagating Type 5 LSAs, NSSAs use Type 7 LSAs to carry external routing information. These Type 7 LSAs are created by an Autonomous System Boundary Router located within the NSSA and are translated into Type 5 LSAs by the ABR when they exit the NSSA and enter the backbone or another OSPF area.

The NSSA design is especially useful in scenarios where a branch office or edge site needs to redistribute external routes, such as static routes or routes from another protocol like RIP, into OSPF, but still benefits from the reduced complexity of a stub configuration. NSSA provides a compromise, allowing the redistribution to occur without flooding the area with Type 5 LSAs. It preserves the simplicity of a stub while offering the functionality of route injection. Like stub areas, all routers in the NSSA must be configured to recognize the area as NSSA; otherwise, they will fail to form adjacencies and will not function correctly in the OSPF domain.

A further enhancement of NSSA is the totally NSSA, similar in principle to the totally stubby area. In a totally NSSA, Type 3 LSAs are also suppressed, and only a default route is provided in addition to the locally originated Type 7 LSAs. This setup is advantageous in small remote offices that need to originate external routes while using only default routes for all other destinations. It provides a high degree of simplification and control, which is ideal for lightweight routing environments.

From a configuration standpoint, defining an area as stub or NSSA involves router-level commands that are specific to each vendor but generally straightforward. In Cisco IOS, for example, the area [area-id] stub or area [area-id] nssa command is issued under the OSPF routing process, and additional keywords can be added to define totally stubby or totally NSSA behavior. In Juniper and MikroTik systems, similar capabilities exist, though the syntax and logic may vary slightly. Regardless of platform, proper configuration and consistency across all routers in the area are essential to ensure reliable operation.

It is important to understand the limitations of stub and NSSA areas. Since stub areas do not accept external routes, they are not suitable for placement of ASBRs unless the area is NSSA. Also, summarization of routes into stub areas must be done with care to avoid reachability problems. While these area types simplify routing and reduce overhead, they also limit visibility and control, which may impact advanced routing policies or traffic engineering efforts. Their use should be carefully considered during the network design phase, especially in environments that require redundancy, failover, or diverse exit points for internet access.

Stub and NSSA areas are powerful features in OSPF that enhance the protocol's scalability, efficiency, and manageability. They help administrators tailor routing behavior to the specific needs of each segment of the network, reducing unnecessary information while preserving essential connectivity. In well-designed OSPF topologies, these area types can significantly improve performance and reduce complexity, especially in networks with a clear distinction between core, distribution, and access layers. By understanding how stub and NSSA areas function and where to deploy them, network engineers can build OSPF domains that are both robust and resource-efficient, capable of adapting to the demands of modern enterprise and service provider environments.

Chapter 13: OSPF Troubleshooting Techniques

OSPF is a dynamic and sophisticated routing protocol, capable of handling large and complex topologies through its hierarchical design and link-state operation. However, like any routing protocol, OSPF can encounter issues that disrupt communication, cause routing inconsistencies, or lead to network outages. Troubleshooting OSPF requires a methodical approach and a solid understanding of the protocol's operation, including neighbor relationships, area design, route propagation, LSA types, and path selection based on cost metrics. Knowing where to look and what to analyze is essential for resolving issues quickly and efficiently, especially in environments where uptime is critical.

The first and most fundamental aspect of OSPF troubleshooting is verifying the formation of neighbor adjacencies. OSPF routers must first establish neighbor relationships before exchanging routing information. If two routers on the same network segment are not becoming neighbors, the issue often lies in the Hello packet exchange.

This is where the investigation should begin. Administrators should check whether Hello packets are being sent and received. A mismatch in configuration parameters such as Hello interval, Dead interval, area ID, authentication settings, or network type will prevent adjacency from forming. Using interface-specific commands, logs, or debugs can reveal whether Hello packets are being exchanged and whether the neighbor state is progressing beyond the Init or Two-Way stage.

The next step in troubleshooting is to examine the OSPF neighbor states. OSPF follows a series of well-defined states when forming an adjacency, from Down to Init, Two-Way, ExStart, Exchange, Loading, and finally Full. Each of these states reflects a particular stage in the synchronization of link-state databases. If routers are stuck in ExStart or Exchange, there may be issues with MTU mismatches, which can prevent database description packets from being acknowledged properly. Inconsistent MTU settings on the interfaces of OSPF neighbors are a common cause of stuck states. Adjusting the MTU to match on both sides or using the OSPF interface command to ignore MTU mismatches can help resolve this issue.

Another critical element of OSPF troubleshooting is verifying that the area configuration is consistent. All interfaces participating in OSPF must be assigned to an area, and all routers within the same area must agree on the area type. If a router attempts to form an adjacency with another router in a different area, the adjacency will fail. This also applies to special area types such as stub and NSSA. If one router is configured as a stub and its neighbor is not, they will not become neighbors. Ensuring that all routers within an area share the same configuration is essential for proper OSPF operation.

After confirming that neighbors are formed and adjacencies are established, attention should turn to the link-state database. OSPF relies on LSAs to describe the topology of the network. Routers exchange LSAs to populate their databases and compute the shortest path tree using Dijkstra's algorithm. Problems with LSA propagation can lead to incomplete or inconsistent routing tables. Using diagnostic commands to view the LSDB, administrators can check whether all expected LSAs are present and whether the database is synchronized with neighbors. Missing LSAs can indicate filtering issues, network type mismatches, or interface problems that prevent LSAs from being generated or flooded correctly.

Interface issues are another common source of OSPF problems. If an interface participating in OSPF goes down or becomes unstable, it can cause routes to be withdrawn or LSAs to be flushed from the database. Monitoring interface status, checking for physical errors, and reviewing interface counters can help identify whether the root cause lies in the underlying transport. Interfaces must also be assigned the correct OSPF network type, as this influences how OSPF forms adjacencies and floods LSAs. Misconfigured network types, such as assigning point-to-point to a broadcast segment or vice versa, can lead to unexpected behavior, including failed adjacencies or improper DR/BDR elections.

DR and BDR election problems can also disrupt OSPF operation, particularly on broadcast and non-broadcast multi-access networks. If multiple routers are on the same segment, OSPF will elect one as the Designated Router and another as the Backup Designated Router. All other routers will form adjacencies with the DR and BDR but not with each other. Misunderstandings in this process can cause routers to remain in the Two-Way state, never reaching Full adjacency. Adjusting OSPF priority values or explicitly setting which routers should become DR or BDR can help control the election process and ensure stable operation.

Route filtering and summarization are additional areas to inspect during troubleshooting. Incorrectly applied filters or overly aggressive summarization can result in missing routes or routing loops. On ABRs and ASBRs, route summarization must be carefully configured to ensure that the summarized routes accurately reflect the underlying networks. Filters applied using distribute-lists, route-maps, or prefix-lists must also be reviewed to ensure they are not inadvertently blocking necessary prefixes. When a route is missing from the routing table, tracing its path from origin to destination, through all intermediate routers, can help identify where it was filtered or dropped.

Another important tool in OSPF troubleshooting is the routing table itself. The routing table shows the final result of the OSPF process and is where all best paths are installed after cost calculations. If an expected route is missing, or if the wrong route is selected, checking the administrative distance, OSPF cost, and presence of competing routes from other protocols is critical. OSPF has a default administrative distance of 110, and if another protocol like EIGRP or static routing offers a route to the same destination with a lower administrative distance, it will be preferred. Understanding how OSPF metrics work and comparing costs across paths can explain why one route was chosen over another.

In networks where route redistribution is used, additional care must be taken to verify redistribution policies and tag management. When routes are redistributed into OSPF from another protocol, the origin of the route must be clearly understood, and any route-maps or metrics applied during redistribution must be evaluated. Improper metric assignment or tag conflicts can lead to routing loops or suboptimal routing. Debugging redistribution processes and monitoring the propagation of external LSAs can provide insight into where problems originate.

Using packet captures and OSPF-specific debug commands can be invaluable during deeper troubleshooting. Capturing OSPF packets on an interface can reveal whether Hello packets are being sent, LSAs are being received, and acknowledgments are occurring. Debugging commands provide real-time feedback on OSPF state changes, neighbor activity, LSA generation, and SPF calculations. These tools must be used carefully, especially in production environments, as they can generate significant output and impact performance. However, when used with precision, they allow administrators to gain visibility into the internal workings of OSPF and identify issues that are not obvious through basic commands alone.

Effective OSPF troubleshooting is a blend of protocol knowledge, careful observation, and systematic investigation. Understanding the sequence of OSPF operations and knowing which components to verify at each step allows network engineers to diagnose and resolve problems efficiently. Whether dealing with adjacency failures, missing routes, LSA inconsistencies, or routing loops, a structured approach ensures that root causes are found and resolved without introducing new problems. Mastering OSPF troubleshooting techniques is not just about fixing issues but also about building resilient networks that can withstand change, recover from faults, and deliver reliable performance in the most demanding environments.

Chapter 14: Implementing OSPF in Cisco

Implementing OSPF on Cisco routers is a fundamental skill for network engineers working in enterprise or service provider environments. Cisco's implementation of OSPF follows industry standards defined by the IETF, and it also includes enhancements that improve operational flexibility. Setting up OSPF on Cisco devices involves configuring the OSPF process, defining the router ID, enabling OSPF on interfaces, assigning areas, and optionally fine-tuning parameters for performance, security, and scalability. Cisco routers use IOS as the primary interface for configuration and management, and OSPF can be configured both in traditional CLI mode and in newer configuration models depending on the platform in use.

The starting point for OSPF implementation is enabling the OSPF routing process. In Cisco IOS, this is done using the router ospf [process-id] command in global configuration mode. The process ID is a local identifier and does not need to match on all routers. It is simply used to distinguish between different OSPF processes running on the same router, although in most networks, a single OSPF process per router is sufficient. Once the process is enabled, OSPF can be activated on interfaces by using the network command. This command takes an IP address, a wildcard mask, and an area assignment. The combination of IP address and wildcard mask determines which interfaces participate in OSPF and into which area they are placed.

For example, to enable OSPF on interfaces in the 192.168.1.0/24 network and assign them to Area 0, the command would be network 192.168.1.0 0.0.0.255 area 0. The wildcard mask is the inverse of the subnet mask, so a /24 subnet uses 0.0.0.255. It is important to understand that the network command in Cisco OSPF configuration is not about advertising specific routes but about identifying which interfaces should run OSPF. The router checks its local interfaces and

49

compares them against the network statements. Any matching interfaces are enabled for OSPF, and Hello packets begin to be sent.

Another critical configuration step is setting the router ID. The router ID is a 32-bit value that uniquely identifies the OSPF router within the domain. By default, the router ID is chosen based on the highest IP address on a loopback interface. If no loopbacks are configured, the highest active physical interface IP is used. However, it is best practice to manually configure the router ID using the router-id [ip-address] command under the OSPF process. A manually configured router ID provides consistency and predictability, especially when troubleshooting or viewing topology databases, where router IDs are used to identify LSA origins and OSPF neighbors.

Once basic OSPF is configured, neighbor relationships will form automatically on broadcast interfaces such as Ethernet, as long as Hello packets are received and essential parameters match. These parameters include the Hello interval, Dead interval, area ID, authentication settings, and stub flags. If these values are not consistent between two routers, the adjacency will fail. Cisco IOS provides detailed verification commands such as show ip ospf neighbor, which displays the state of each neighbor and helps identify problems in the adjacency process. Other useful commands include show ip ospf interface to view OSPF-enabled interfaces and their parameters, and show ip ospf database to inspect the link-state database.

For more complex topologies, Cisco routers support advanced OSPF features such as multiple areas, summarization, redistribution, and authentication. When using multiple areas, it is necessary to ensure that all non-backbone areas connect to Area 0, either directly or through a virtual link. ABRs are configured by simply having interfaces in more than one area. Summarization can be performed on ABRs using the area [area-id] range [address] [mask] command, allowing the router to advertise summary LSAs to other areas. External route summarization on ASBRs is done using the summary-address command under the redistribution configuration.

Redistribution is another common requirement in Cisco OSPF deployments. When OSPF needs to exchange routes with other protocols such as EIGRP, BGP, or static routes, redistribution is configured using the redistribute command under the OSPF process. Metrics must be set during redistribution since OSPF does not automatically assign them to external routes. The command redistribute static subnets metric-type 1 is an example of injecting static routes as Type 1 external routes. Care must be taken to avoid routing loops or instability when redistributing between protocols, especially in networks with multiple redistribution points.

OSPF authentication on Cisco routers is used to secure OSPF messages and ensure that only trusted routers participate in the routing domain. Cisco supports plain-text and MD5 authentication for OSPFv2. Authentication is configured on a per-interface basis. To enable MD5 authentication, the interface must first be set to use message-digest authentication with the ip ospf authentication message-digest command, followed by the ip ospf message-digest-key [key-id] md5 [password] command to set the key. All routers on the same link must use the same key ID and password for the authentication to work. For OSPFv3, authentication is handled by IPsec, and configuration requires additional steps to define security associations.

Cisco IOS also allows fine-tuning of OSPF timers and behavior. For example, Hello and Dead intervals can be adjusted on an interface to change how frequently Hello packets are sent and how quickly dead neighbors are detected. This is useful in low-latency environments where faster convergence is desired. Commands like ip ospf hello-interval and ip ospf dead-interval are used to set these timers. However, these values must match between neighbors to maintain adjacencies. Cisco routers also support passive interfaces, which allow OSPF to advertise networks without sending Hello packets on an interface. This is commonly used on interfaces that face end hosts rather than other routers.

Cisco's diagnostic and monitoring capabilities further enhance OSPF implementation. Tools such as debugging, logging, and SNMP provide insight into OSPF operations in real time. The debug ip ospf events and debug ip ospf adj commands help trace the neighbor formation process, while debug ip ospf lsa-generation tracks the creation of LSAs. Although powerful, debug commands should be used cautiously in production environments due to their potential impact on router performance.

Implementing OSPF on Cisco routers offers a combination of simplicity and depth. The basic configuration is straightforward, making it accessible for small networks or learners. At the same time, Cisco's implementation supports all advanced OSPF features required for complex enterprise environments. Whether deploying OSPF across a campus, within a data center, or as part of a multi-area WAN, the tools and flexibility provided by Cisco IOS make it possible to build stable, scalable, and secure OSPF topologies. Mastering OSPF implementation in Cisco environments is not only essential for certification but also foundational for real-world network engineering and architecture.

Chapter 15: Implementing OSPF in Juniper

Implementing OSPF in Juniper Networks devices involves a fundamentally different configuration style than Cisco, relying on a structured, hierarchical configuration model based on Junos OS. Juniper routers use a clean and logical format for routing configuration, with a strong focus on separation between routing protocols, interfaces, and routing instances. OSPF in Juniper is implemented under the [edit protocols ospf] hierarchy, and enabling it requires understanding how Junos handles interfaces, areas, and logical units. While the OSPF protocol adheres to the same standards as defined by the IETF, the configuration and operational verification tools in Junos are tailored to provide a powerful yet precise way of managing OSPF behavior in both simple and complex network environments.

The first step in deploying OSPF on a Juniper router is enabling the OSPF protocol itself. In Junos, this is done under the protocols hierarchy, specifically by navigating to [edit protocols ospf]. From there, the administrator can define global parameters such as the router ID, reference bandwidth, and optionally, authentication settings. If a router ID is not manually configured, Junos will automatically select one based on the highest loopback interface IP address or, if none exists, the highest interface IP. However, best practice dictates setting a static router ID using the command set router-id followed by a unique 32-bit address. This ensures consistency in troubleshooting, logging, and LSA generation.

Unlike Cisco, Juniper does not use network statements to activate OSPF on interfaces. Instead, interfaces are explicitly assigned to OSPF areas under the [edit protocols ospf area] hierarchy. Each interface that should participate in OSPF must be specified individually, including the logical unit number, which is almost always unit 0 in most configurations. For example, to enable OSPF on interface ge-0/0/1.0 in Area 0, the configuration would include a line like set protocols ospf area 0.0.0.0 interface ge-0/0/1.0. This precision allows granular control and avoids the ambiguity of wildcard masks. It also means that only those interfaces explicitly listed will participate in OSPF, reducing the likelihood of inadvertently enabling OSPF on unintended interfaces.

OSPF area configuration in Junos follows the standard format, where the backbone area is designated as 0.0.0.0, and other areas use dotted-decimal identifiers. Within each area, options such as stub area type or NSSA configuration can be specified. For instance, configuring an area as a stub involves adding the stub statement under that area's hierarchy. When using multiple areas, Juniper routers automatically act as Area Border Routers when they have interfaces in more than one area. Unlike some Cisco implementations, there is no need to explicitly define the role of a router as an ABR; it is derived from the configuration.

Authentication in Juniper is also interface-specific and supports both simple and MD5 authentication. To enable MD5 authentication, a key is configured on the interface under the OSPF area. This involves setting the authentication type to md5 and specifying a key ID and password. The configuration ensures that only routers with matching keys can form adjacencies. This is essential in shared network segments where security is a concern. Authentication mismatches in Junos will prevent neighbor formation, and logs will indicate authentication errors if present. In mission-critical networks or multi-tenant environments, authentication is an important layer of security and should always be considered part of standard OSPF deployment.

Juniper provides excellent tools for verifying and troubleshooting OSPF configuration and operation. The show ospf neighbor command displays the list of OSPF neighbors, their states, designated router election results, and interface details. The show ospf interface command provides details on OSPF-enabled interfaces, including the Hello and Dead intervals, cost, and neighbor status. The link-state database can be viewed using show ospf database, which shows all LSAs the router has learned or originated. These outputs are well structured and allow network engineers to quickly diagnose adjacency issues, topology inconsistencies, or routing problems.

Route propagation in Juniper is tightly integrated with the Routing Engine and the Routing Information Base. Once OSPF has learned about network prefixes, these are installed in the routing table if they are deemed the best path. Junos supports route preferences, with OSPF internal routes having a default preference of 10, while external routes have a higher preference, such as 150. Preference values in Junos serve the same purpose as administrative distance in Cisco IOS. They determine which route to install when multiple routing protocols advertise the same destination. Adjusting these preferences can influence route selection and is sometimes necessary in multi-protocol environments where OSPF competes with BGP, RIP, or static routes.

For more advanced deployments, Junos supports route summarization on Area Border Routers. Summarization is configured under the [edit protocols ospf area] section using the range statement. This allows a router to advertise a summary route into another area, reducing the number of LSAs and keeping the OSPF database compact. When redistributing external routes from other protocols into OSPF, Juniper routers support the use of policy statements to filter and modify route attributes. Redistribution is configured under the OSPF protocol hierarchy with export policies that match routes and define how they are advertised. These policies provide a powerful and flexible mechanism to control OSPF route advertisement and support complex policy-based routing logic.

Juniper also supports virtual links when a non-backbone area needs to connect to Area 0 but has no direct physical path. Virtual links are configured under the backbone area and specify the remote router ID and transit area. They function as logical tunnels that allow OSPF to maintain backbone continuity. While virtual links are sometimes necessary, they are best used as a temporary solution, as they add complexity and can complicate troubleshooting. A more stable design involves ensuring all non-backbone areas connect directly to Area 0 through physical or logical topologies.

Junos includes options to fine-tune OSPF performance, including adjusting Hello and Dead intervals, interface cost, and passive interfaces. The passive interface setting disables OSPF Hello packets on an interface while still advertising the network. This is useful on interfaces connected to end hosts or where no OSPF neighbors exist. Cost values can be manually set on interfaces to influence path selection. Since OSPF chooses the lowest cost path, adjusting the cost can be used to manipulate routing behavior, load balance traffic, or create backup paths.

In real-world deployments, Juniper's robust OSPF implementation is trusted for its clarity, stability, and extensibility. It is used in data centers, service provider networks, and enterprise WANs where precise routing behavior and high availability are required. The combination of a structured configuration model, powerful policy engine, and intuitive operational commands makes Junos an ideal platform for OSPF deployment. Engineers familiar with the protocol's theory will find Juniper's implementation logical and efficient, with all the tools necessary to design and maintain reliable and scalable OSPF-based networks.

Chapter 16: Implementing OSPF in MikroTik

MikroTik routers, powered by RouterOS, provide a full-featured and flexible platform for deploying dynamic routing protocols, including OSPF. Implementing OSPF on MikroTik devices involves working through the Winbox graphical interface, WebFig, or the terminal CLI, each offering the same functionality with different interaction styles. OSPF is part of the MikroTik routing package, and once enabled, it offers comprehensive support for link-state routing in a variety of network topologies. While the foundational principles of OSPF remain the same across all vendors, the approach and configuration logic in MikroTik are tailored to the RouterOS design philosophy, which emphasizes a modular and interface-based routing model.

Before configuring OSPF on a MikroTik router, the first step is to ensure the routing package is installed and active. On modern versions of RouterOS, routing protocols like OSPF are typically included by default, but verifying this through the Packages menu ensures the necessary components are present. Once confirmed, OSPF configuration begins in the Routing section, under the OSPF submenu. MikroTik separates OSPF into several parts, including Instances, Areas, Networks, Interfaces, and Neighbors. Understanding how these pieces fit together is essential for a successful and efficient implementation.

The configuration begins by defining an OSPF instance. The instance contains global parameters for OSPF operation, such as the router ID and the routing table in use. If not manually set, the router ID will be automatically assigned based on the highest IP address configured on an active interface. However, it is best practice to explicitly configure the router ID to ensure consistent and predictable behavior across the network. Setting a static router ID prevents changes in routing behavior during interface state transitions or IP reassignments, which can otherwise trigger unnecessary SPF calculations or LSA flooding.

Next, the OSPF area must be defined. The backbone area, as per OSPF standards, is always designated as area ID 0.0.0.0. Additional areas can be configured as needed, particularly in larger deployments where hierarchy and summarization are necessary. Each area can be configured with options such as stub or NSSA, depending on the network design. MikroTik allows each OSPF interface or network to be assigned to a specific area, enabling effective control of topology segmentation. Stub areas can be used to limit Type 5 LSA propagation, while NSSA areas permit the injection of external routes using Type 7 LSAs, ideal for branch offices or edge networks with local internet or external protocol redistribution.

After defining areas, OSPF must be enabled on the appropriate interfaces. MikroTik allows administrators to bind OSPF to interfaces directly or define networks using the Networks menu. In the Networks section, the administrator specifies the IP prefix and the area to which the network belongs. When the router finds a match between a local IP interface and a defined network prefix, it activates OSPF on that interface. Alternatively, in the Interfaces section, administrators can manually associate an interface with an OSPF instance and configure its properties. This flexibility allows for precise control over which interfaces participate in OSPF and how they behave.

MikroTik also provides support for DR and BDR elections on broadcast and NBMA networks. Interfaces can be tuned using options such as priority, Hello interval, and Dead interval. The interface priority influences which router becomes the DR or BDR, and adjusting it is essential when deterministic elections are required. Hello and Dead intervals must match between OSPF peers for adjacencies to form. These timers can be configured per interface to control the sensitivity of neighbor failure detection. Faster timers result in quicker convergence but can increase CPU utilization and sensitivity to minor interruptions, while longer timers reduce overhead but delay route recalculations.

Authentication is another critical component in OSPF deployment, especially in environments where multiple routers share the same segment or when OSPF is running over untrusted links. MikroTik supports both plain-text and MD5 authentication. To configure authentication, it must first be enabled in the Area settings. Then, under the Interfaces section, a password or MD5 key is defined. All routers on the same link must share the same authentication settings for adjacencies to be established. Proper implementation of authentication ensures that only authorized routers can exchange routing information and prevents the injection of false LSAs.

Redistribution into OSPF is possible through the Redistribution submenu, allowing static routes, connected routes, or routes from other routing protocols to be advertised in OSPF. MikroTik supports setting the metric type for redistributed routes, distinguishing between E1 and E2 external routes. E2 is the default and does not include the internal OSPF cost to the ASBR, while E1 includes the internal cost and is more reflective of the actual path. When controlling route redistribution, administrators can apply filters to prevent unwanted prefixes from entering the OSPF domain, avoiding unnecessary LSA overhead and improving routing clarity.

To monitor and troubleshoot OSPF, MikroTik offers several diagnostic tools. The Neighbors submenu displays the list of OSPF neighbors and their current state, including DR and BDR roles. The Routes menu shows OSPF-learned routes, including the metric and route type. The LSAs menu provides visibility into the link-state database, including the origin of LSAs and their age. For real-time diagnostics, MikroTik supports logging OSPF events and using packet sniffing or Torch to analyze Hello packets and LSA exchanges. These tools are indispensable for resolving adjacency issues, route propagation problems, or performance anomalies.

When designing OSPF networks with MikroTik, it is essential to adhere to best practices such as assigning loopback interfaces for stable router IDs, planning area structure to allow summarization and scalability, and securing OSPF exchanges with authentication. Loopback interfaces provide a logical and consistent endpoint for OSPF identification, improving redundancy and stability. Hierarchical area design allows for route summarization and limits the impact of network changes. OSPF supports summarization at area boundaries, which can be configured in the Instances submenu. Proper use of summarization reduces the number of LSAs and enhances overall network convergence performance.

In multi-router or multi-vendor environments, MikroTik's adherence to OSPF standards ensures interoperability with Cisco, Juniper, and other networking platforms. As long as the core OSPF principles are respected, such as matching area IDs, Hello intervals, and authentication, MikroTik devices can seamlessly integrate into existing OSPF domains. This makes MikroTik a powerful choice for edge deployments, branch connectivity, or even as part of the OSPF backbone in cost-conscious environments. The blend of affordability, feature richness, and standards compliance allows MikroTik to deliver enterprise-grade dynamic routing capabilities without the complexity or licensing constraints found in some other platforms.

Implementing OSPF in MikroTik devices is both intuitive and robust, providing a rich set of features through a well-organized interface.

Whether using CLI for automation and scripting or the GUI for ease of management, administrators can deploy, monitor, and optimize OSPF to meet the needs of modern networks. By mastering the nuances of MikroTik's OSPF implementation, network engineers can build scalable, secure, and efficient routing domains capable of adapting to growth, redundancy requirements, and ever-evolving topological demands.

Chapter 17: EIGRP Fundamentals and Concepts

Enhanced Interior Gateway Routing Protocol, commonly known as EIGRP, is a hybrid routing protocol developed by Cisco Systems. It combines the characteristics of both distance-vector and link-state routing protocols, making it one of the most efficient and flexible dynamic routing protocols used in enterprise networks. EIGRP was originally proprietary to Cisco, but a partial version was later released to the IETF, allowing limited multi-vendor interoperability. Its hybrid nature allows it to achieve faster convergence than traditional distance-vector protocols like RIP, while maintaining simpler configuration and resource efficiency compared to more complex link-state protocols like OSPF. Understanding the fundamentals and concepts of EIGRP provides the necessary foundation for implementing and optimizing routing in Cisco-based environments.

At the core of EIGRP is the use of the Diffusing Update Algorithm, or DUAL. This algorithm is responsible for ensuring loop-free and efficient route calculations. DUAL maintains a topology table for each EIGRP-enabled router, storing information about all available routes received from neighbors, including the feasible distance and advertised distance for each path. Unlike traditional distance-vector protocols, which only maintain a single best route, EIGRP keeps track of multiple routes and evaluates their feasibility based on strict conditions. This allows for rapid convergence and the ability to maintain backup paths that can be used immediately if the primary route fails.

EIGRP classifies routes using several terms, the most important of which are feasible distance, advertised distance, successor, and feasible successor. The feasible distance is the lowest calculated metric to reach a destination, including the cost to the neighbor advertising the route. The advertised distance is the metric reported by the neighbor to reach the destination. A successor is the next-hop router for the best path to a destination, and this route is placed in the routing table. A feasible successor is a backup route that satisfies the feasibility condition, which requires that its advertised distance be less than the current feasible distance. This rule ensures loop-free backups are available and can be used instantly when needed, without triggering a full recomputation of the topology.

EIGRP uses a composite metric that considers bandwidth, delay, reliability, and load. By default, only bandwidth and delay are used, with the other components available if configured. The metric calculation is controlled by a set of values called K-values, which can be adjusted to influence route selection. However, K-values must be consistent across all routers in an EIGRP domain, or neighbor adjacencies will fail to form. The use of multiple parameters in the metric calculation allows EIGRP to make more intelligent routing decisions based on link characteristics rather than simple hop count, as seen in RIP.

Neighbor relationships in EIGRP are established by sending Hello packets to directly connected routers. These Hello packets are multicast by default and contain information such as the autonomous system number, hold time, and EIGRP version. If two routers receive each other's Hello packets and their parameters match, they become neighbors and begin exchanging routing information. Unlike OSPF, EIGRP does not require full adjacency with every neighbor on a segment, and there are no DR or BDR elections. Once neighbors are established, EIGRP routers exchange updates only when there is a change in the network topology, rather than periodic full updates. This behavior reduces bandwidth usage and processing overhead.

EIGRP uses three main tables to manage routing: the neighbor table, the topology table, and the routing table. The neighbor table lists all directly connected EIGRP neighbors and is maintained through the exchange of Hello packets. The topology table stores all learned routes, including successors and feasible successors, and their associated metrics. This table is used by the DUAL algorithm to select the best routes. The routing table contains the final result of the selection process and is used to forward traffic. These separate tables allow EIGRP to operate efficiently, quickly respond to changes, and maintain a high degree of route stability.

One of EIGRP's strengths is its support for unequal-cost load balancing. Unlike most routing protocols, which only support equal-cost multipath routing, EIGRP can use multiple paths with different metrics to reach the same destination, as long as they meet a configurable variance threshold. This allows more efficient use of available bandwidth and supports more granular traffic distribution across redundant links. The variance command is used to specify how much worse a secondary path's metric can be compared to the best path while still being considered for routing.

EIGRP also supports route summarization at any interface, which helps reduce the size of routing tables and limits the scope of topology changes. Manual summarization is configured on a per-interface basis, and summary routes can include multiple subnets, reducing the number of individual routes that must be advertised and processed. This contributes to network stability and scalability, especially in large deployments. Additionally, EIGRP supports automatic summarization in older versions, though this behavior is disabled by default in modern configurations due to its potential to cause reachability issues in discontiguous networks.

In addition to IPv4, EIGRP supports IPv6, where it operates in much the same way, but with interface-based configuration rather than network statements. In EIGRP for IPv6, autonomous system numbers and router IDs must be explicitly defined, and routes are exchanged using link-local addresses. This makes the configuration slightly different but conceptually consistent with EIGRP for IPv4. IPv6 support ensures that EIGRP remains relevant in modern networks transitioning to the next generation of IP addressing.

EIGRP also offers robust filtering and route control mechanisms. Route filtering can be performed using prefix-lists, route-maps, or distribute-lists, allowing administrators to control which routes are advertised, accepted, or installed. This level of control is crucial in complex topologies, where routing policies must be enforced to support traffic engineering, security boundaries, or administrative segmentation.

As a protocol, EIGRP is known for its fast convergence, low overhead, and ease of configuration, making it ideal for enterprise networks where performance and flexibility are priorities. Its ability to rapidly adapt to changes without consuming excessive resources makes it especially well-suited for environments that include remote branches, redundant WAN links, and mixed topologies. By combining the best features of distance-vector and link-state protocols, EIGRP provides a balance of speed, scalability, and simplicity that continues to make it a preferred choice among Cisco professionals and network architects. Understanding EIGRP fundamentals is not only important for certification but also for designing reliable and adaptive routing strategies in the real world.

Chapter 18: EIGRP Packet Types and Operation

Enhanced Interior Gateway Routing Protocol, or EIGRP, uses a set of specialized packet types to establish and maintain neighbor relationships, exchange routing information, and ensure network convergence. Unlike older distance-vector protocols that rely on periodic updates, EIGRP uses a more intelligent, event-driven communication model based on the Diffusing Update Algorithm. This model allows routers to exchange information only when necessary, minimizing bandwidth usage and reducing convergence time. Understanding how EIGRP communicates through its packet types is essential for analyzing its operation and for troubleshooting network issues effectively.

EIGRP operates primarily using five packet types: Hello, Acknowledgment, Update, Query, and Reply. Each serves a distinct purpose within the protocol's logic and is critical for maintaining a reliable and loop-free routing environment. These packets are encapsulated using Reliable Transport Protocol, a Cisco proprietary transport mechanism that ensures guaranteed delivery of EIGRP messages. RTP allows for both multicast and unicast communication, offering efficiency when sending updates to multiple neighbors and reliability when delivering critical messages to specific routers.

The Hello packet is the foundation of EIGRP neighbor establishment. These packets are sent at regular intervals out of EIGRP-enabled interfaces to discover and maintain neighbor relationships. Hello packets are multicast by default using the address 224.0.0.10 for IPv4 and FF02::A for IPv6. They include information such as the autonomous system number, hold time, K-values, and source router ID. When a router receives a Hello packet from another EIGRP-speaking router on a shared segment, it compares the parameters in the packet to its own configuration. If the values are compatible, including matching K-values and AS number, and the source IP is reachable, the router considers the sender a neighbor and adds it to the EIGRP neighbor table. The hold time determines how long the router should wait before declaring the neighbor unreachable if no further Hello packets are received. This timer plays a critical role in neighbor stability and network convergence.

Once neighbor relationships are established through Hello packets, the routers can begin exchanging routing information. This is done using Update packets. EIGRP Update packets are used to transmit routing information to new neighbors and to communicate route changes when topology changes occur. Unlike distance-vector protocols that send the entire routing table periodically, EIGRP sends only incremental updates, and only to routers that need the information. When a new neighbor is discovered, the router sends all of its known routes in Update packets. These updates are sent reliably using RTP, and acknowledgment is required for each Update packet to confirm receipt. If an acknowledgment is not received within a certain timeframe, the packet is retransmitted. This reliable delivery ensures consistency and synchronization between routers.

Acknowledgment packets in EIGRP are used to confirm the receipt of Update, Query, and Reply packets. They are always sent using unicast and do not contain any routing information. Acknowledgment packets are essential for the reliability of the protocol. Since EIGRP uses RTP instead of relying on TCP or UDP, it must implement its own mechanisms for reliable message delivery. Acknowledgments help maintain the integrity of the communication process and ensure that every packet exchange is accounted for.

Query packets play a vital role in EIGRP's loop prevention and fast convergence. When a route becomes unavailable and there is no feasible successor to immediately take over, EIGRP enters an active state for that destination. The router sends Query packets to all of its neighbors, asking if they have a path to the unreachable destination. These queries are sent reliably and must be acknowledged. This process begins a distributed computation using the DUAL algorithm to discover an alternative path. Query packets essentially initiate a network-wide search for a new route, and they help ensure that every router in the network has consistent knowledge of the topology. This mechanism is one of the key differences between EIGRP and simpler protocols like RIP, which rely solely on timers to expire routes and discover new ones.

When a router receives a Query and has an alternate path to the destination, it responds with a Reply packet. If it does not have an alternate route, it also forwards the Query to its own neighbors, continuing the process. Once a suitable replacement route is found or the search has been exhausted, the router sends Reply packets to the original sender. EIGRP does not consider a route converged until it has received replies from all queried neighbors. This ensures that no routing loops are formed and that all routers have a synchronized view of the network. The Reply packet, like the Update and Query packets, is sent reliably and must be acknowledged. This controlled process of querying and replying is fundamental to EIGRP's capability for rapid, loop-free convergence.

Another important feature of EIGRP's operation is its use of bounded updates. Unlike protocols that flood the network with updates, EIGRP sends route changes only to those neighbors that are affected. If a topology change occurs that does not influence a certain neighbor's routing decisions, that neighbor receives no update. This behavior minimizes unnecessary traffic and helps conserve bandwidth, especially in large-scale environments with many routers and links. Bounded updates, combined with reliable transport and triggered communication, give EIGRP an efficiency advantage over both traditional distance-vector and complex link-state protocols.

EIGRP also employs route filtering and route summarization as part of its operational model. While these are not packet types, they influence how routing information is propagated and can directly affect which routes are included in Update or Query packets. Summarization can be configured on a per-interface basis, allowing administrators to control the granularity of route advertisements. This leads to fewer updates, smaller routing tables, and faster convergence during changes. Route filtering, when implemented using distribute-lists or route-maps, can suppress certain routes from being advertised or accepted, adding another layer of policy-based control to the protocol's operation.

EIGRP's packet-based communication model, supported by the Reliable Transport Protocol, allows it to be both efficient and dependable. Each packet type has a specific role in maintaining neighbor relationships, synchronizing routing databases, and facilitating rapid, loop-free convergence. This intelligent use of Hello, Acknowledgment, Update, Query, and Reply packets ensures that EIGRP can respond quickly to topology changes without overwhelming the network with unnecessary traffic. By understanding how these packets work together, network engineers can better design, monitor, and troubleshoot EIGRP-based networks, ensuring that they remain robust, scalable, and high-performing even under dynamic conditions.

Chapter 19: EIGRP Metric Calculation and K-values

The metric calculation in EIGRP is one of the features that sets it apart from many other routing protocols. Unlike RIP, which uses a simple hop count, or OSPF, which uses interface bandwidth to calculate cost, EIGRP uses a composite metric that takes into account several characteristics of a path. These include bandwidth, delay, reliability, and load. Each of these components can be weighted using values known as K-values, which control the influence of each metric in the final path selection process. This multi-faceted approach gives EIGRP the ability to make more informed routing decisions that better reflect the real-world performance and characteristics of the network infrastructure.

The EIGRP composite metric is calculated using a formula that involves five K-values, traditionally labeled K1 through K5. These K-values are configurable and determine which components of the metric formula are active and how much influence each has. The default values used in most EIGRP deployments are K1 and K3 set to 1, while K2, K4, and K5 are set to 0. With this default configuration, EIGRP uses only bandwidth and delay in the metric calculation, ignoring reliability and load unless the administrator specifically enables them. This default configuration balances simplicity and performance while providing enough intelligence to make accurate and efficient routing decisions.

The bandwidth metric is derived from the minimum bandwidth of the path, expressed in kilobits per second. EIGRP does not average the bandwidth across all links in the path but instead considers only the slowest link. This design reflects the principle that the slowest link in a path is often the limiting factor for throughput. To calculate the bandwidth component of the metric, EIGRP uses the formula 10,000,000 divided by the minimum bandwidth in kilobits per second, which produces a value that increases as the bandwidth decreases. This inverse relationship ensures that higher-bandwidth paths receive a lower metric and are therefore preferred.

The delay component of the EIGRP metric is the cumulative delay of all links along the path, measured in tens of microseconds. Each interface has a configured delay value, which can be manually adjusted to influence routing decisions. EIGRP sums the delay values of all outgoing interfaces in the path and includes this total in the metric calculation. Because delay is additive, it reflects the total latency a packet would experience when traversing the path. This makes it a useful metric for routing decisions in latency-sensitive applications, such as voice over IP or real-time video communication.

When using the default K-values, the final metric is calculated using the formula: metric = 256 × (bandwidth + delay). The multiplication by 256 is an internal scaling factor used by EIGRP to create a more granular metric space and prevent metric collisions. This scaled metric is stored in the topology table and used to compare multiple paths to the same destination. The path with the lowest metric is selected as the successor, or the primary route, and installed in the routing table. Other feasible paths with higher metrics may be retained as feasible successors if they meet the feasibility condition, providing immediate failover in case the primary path fails.

In environments where greater precision or dynamic decision-making is required, administrators may choose to enable additional K-values. K_2 activates the load metric, which reflects the current utilization of the link. K_4 and K_5 relate to reliability, which measures the consistency of the link based on historical error rates. Load and reliability are dynamic metrics, meaning they can change over time based on network conditions. While enabling these metrics may provide more responsive path selection, it also introduces instability because frequent metric changes can trigger route recalculations and convergence events. For this reason, most network engineers leave K_2, K_4, and K_5 at zero and rely on the more stable bandwidth and delay metrics.

Changing K-values across a network must be done with extreme care. All routers participating in the same EIGRP autonomous system must use identical K-values. If a router with different K-values attempts to establish an EIGRP neighbor relationship, the adjacency will fail. This is a safeguard built into EIGRP to ensure consistent metric calculations and prevent routing loops. Before changing any K-values, network engineers must ensure that all routers in the EIGRP domain are updated simultaneously. Coordination, documentation, and testing are critical when implementing such changes to avoid connectivity issues and service disruptions.

In addition to adjusting K-values, EIGRP allows administrators to manipulate metric values manually using interface configurations. Each interface can be configured with a custom bandwidth and delay, allowing the network designer to influence path selection based on topology, design intent, or traffic engineering requirements. For example, increasing the delay on a backup link can discourage its use under normal conditions while still keeping it available as a fallback route. This method provides a more granular level of control than simply changing K-values and is often preferred in production environments.

EIGRP also supports offset lists, which allow administrators to artificially increase the metric for routes learned from specific neighbors. By applying an offset list, the router can influence route selection without modifying physical interface parameters. Offset lists are typically used for policy-based routing scenarios, where traffic must follow a specific path due to business, security, or operational policies. This technique is particularly useful in dual-homed or multi-path environments, where multiple paths to a destination exist, but one path is preferred over another for non-technical reasons.

Understanding the role of K-values and metric calculation in EIGRP is essential for designing networks that behave predictably and efficiently. By controlling the components of the composite metric, network engineers can fine-tune routing behavior to match the needs of the business, the characteristics of the network infrastructure, and the demands of the applications running over it. Whether keeping to the default bandwidth and delay model or enabling more dynamic metrics like load and reliability, the power of EIGRP lies in its ability to adapt routing decisions based on detailed knowledge of link performance. This adaptability, combined with the protocol's fast convergence and support for features like unequal-cost load balancing, makes EIGRP a uniquely flexible solution for enterprise routing.

Chapter 20: EIGRP Neighbor Relationship

The establishment and maintenance of neighbor relationships in EIGRP are essential for the operation of the protocol. Without neighbor adjacencies, routers cannot exchange routing information or maintain awareness of the network topology. EIGRP uses a process that is efficient and intelligent, relying on the exchange of Hello packets and the verification of matching parameters between devices. The resulting neighbor relationships form the basis for all routing activity in EIGRP, from route exchange to topology changes and convergence. Understanding how EIGRP routers discover neighbors, maintain communication, and detect failures is fundamental to building stable and resilient EIGRP-based networks.

EIGRP uses Hello packets to discover and maintain communication with neighboring routers. These packets are sent periodically on all EIGRP-enabled interfaces. By default, they are multicast to the address 224.0.0.10 in IPv4 or FF02::A in IPv6. When a router receives a Hello packet on an interface, it processes the information within the packet and determines whether the sending router meets the criteria to become a neighbor. These criteria include having the same autonomous system number, matching K-values, compatible timers such as Hello and Hold intervals, and a valid interface configuration. If all conditions are met, the router adds the sender to its neighbor table and establishes a bidirectional adjacency.

The neighbor table in EIGRP is a dynamic list of all routers that are directly reachable and have successfully exchanged Hello packets. Each entry in the neighbor table includes the IP address of the neighbor, the interface through which it was learned, the uptime of the adjacency, the sequence number of messages exchanged, and the round-trip time to the neighbor. This table is constantly updated as Hello packets are received. If a neighbor fails to send Hello packets within the agreed-upon Hold time, the router assumes the neighbor is unreachable and removes the entry from the table. This triggers the DUAL algorithm to begin route recalculation if the lost neighbor was contributing to any routing paths.

EIGRP does not require a full mesh of neighbor relationships on multi-access networks. Each router forms neighbor relationships independently with other routers it discovers on a segment. There are no elections for a designated router or backup designated router, unlike OSPF. This simplifies neighbor formation and reduces complexity. However, in large-scale environments, the number of adjacencies can still become significant, especially on broadcast domains such as Ethernet. Careful design using passive interfaces and interface-level filtering can help manage and control neighbor relationships effectively.

One of the most important conditions for neighbor adjacency is the autonomous system number. EIGRP routers must be configured with the same autonomous system number to become neighbors. This number identifies a specific EIGRP routing domain. If two routers have different autonomous system numbers, they will not form a neighbor relationship, even if they are otherwise compatible. The autonomous system boundary also defines where redistribution is needed if multiple EIGRP domains must exchange routes. Within a single domain, EIGRP handles routing natively, using its own metric and topology calculations without requiring redistribution.

K-values must also match between routers for neighbor relationships to form. These values determine how EIGRP calculates its composite metric. If one router is using bandwidth and delay while another is using bandwidth, delay, and load, their metrics will be incompatible. To prevent routing loops and inconsistent route selection, EIGRP will not allow neighbors with mismatched K-values to form adjacencies. This strict requirement ensures consistent metric calculations across the network. When troubleshooting failed adjacencies, mismatched K-values are one of the most common culprits, and verifying them should always be part of the diagnostic process.

EIGRP Hello and Hold timers are additional parameters that influence neighbor relationships. The Hello timer determines how frequently Hello packets are sent, while the Hold timer defines how long a router waits before declaring a neighbor down if no Hello packets are received. These timers must be compatible between routers, but they do not need to be identical. As long as a router receives Hello packets before the Hold timer expires, the relationship remains valid. Adjusting these timers can help optimize convergence and sensitivity to link failures. In high-speed, stable environments, shorter timers can improve responsiveness. In slower or less reliable links, longer timers reduce the risk of false neighbor loss.

Once a neighbor relationship is established, EIGRP begins the process of exchanging routing information. This process is triggered only when a new neighbor is discovered or when a topology change occurs. EIGRP uses Update packets to send route information, and these updates are acknowledged by the receiving router. The use of reliable transport ensures that all routing updates are received and processed in order. Only the necessary information is exchanged, and only with the routers that need it, thanks to EIGRP's use of bounded updates and selective dissemination. This efficiency helps maintain low bandwidth usage and fast convergence.

If a router loses a neighbor, it must recalculate any routes that depended on that neighbor. If a feasible successor is available in the topology table, EIGRP can switch to it immediately, maintaining continuous network connectivity. If no feasible successor exists, the route enters an active state, and the router sends Query packets to all its remaining neighbors to find an alternative path. These packets are processed using the DUAL algorithm, and the router waits for Reply messages from all neighbors before selecting a new route. This mechanism allows EIGRP to converge quickly while avoiding routing loops, even in complex network topologies.

In scenarios where neighbor relationships are unstable or fail to form, administrators must verify a number of configuration elements. These include IP addressing, subnet masks, interface types, K-values, autonomous system numbers, and timer settings. Additionally, features like passive interfaces, access control lists, and route filters can block Hello packets and prevent neighbor formation. Monitoring tools such as show ip eigrp neighbors provide valuable insight into the status of neighbor relationships, including uptime, sequence numbers, and retransmissions. Packet captures and debugs can also reveal whether Hello packets are being sent and received as expected.

Stable and reliable neighbor relationships are the backbone of any EIGRP deployment. They enable routers to share information, maintain synchronized topology tables, and adapt to changes in the network with minimal disruption. Proper configuration, consistent parameter values, and careful design are necessary to ensure that these relationships function as intended. By understanding how EIGRP neighbors are discovered, maintained, and leveraged, network engineers can build robust and scalable routing infrastructures that take full advantage of EIGRP's capabilities. Whether deployed in a small office or a large enterprise network, maintaining healthy EIGRP neighbor relationships is a critical part of achieving efficient and resilient routing.

Chapter 21: EIGRP Authentication

Authentication is a crucial component in securing dynamic routing protocols, and EIGRP supports authentication mechanisms that help ensure only trusted routers can participate in the routing domain. In a network environment where multiple routers exchange routing updates, the integrity and trustworthiness of those updates are vital. Without authentication, a misconfigured or malicious device could potentially inject false routing information, cause routing loops, or redirect traffic inappropriately. EIGRP authentication allows routers to verify the identity of their neighbors before accepting routing information, thereby reinforcing the stability, reliability, and security of the routing infrastructure.

EIGRP supports both plain text and MD5 authentication, with MD5 being the more secure and commonly used option. When authentication is configured, EIGRP Hello packets include a special field where a password or hash value is inserted. Upon receiving a Hello packet, the router checks this field to determine whether the message is valid. If the authentication value does not match the expected key, the packet is discarded and the neighbor relationship is not established. This prevents unauthorized devices from forming adjacencies and injecting potentially harmful routes into the network.

The configuration of EIGRP authentication is performed on a per-interface basis, which allows for precise control over where authentication is applied. This means different interfaces can use different authentication methods or even different keys if required. This flexibility is especially useful in complex topologies or when migrating from an unauthenticated to an authenticated environment. To configure MD5 authentication, the interface must be told to use message-digest authentication. A key chain must also be defined, which contains the password or shared secret. This key chain can include one or more keys, each with its own identifier and lifetime parameters, allowing administrators to rotate keys without service interruption.

Key rotation is a critical security practice that helps reduce the risk of a compromised key being used maliciously. With EIGRP key chains, administrators can configure multiple keys with specific start and end times. During the transition between keys, routers can accept multiple keys for incoming packets while using a single key for outgoing packets. This overlapping acceptance window allows for seamless rotation, minimizing the risk of neighbor loss due to authentication mismatch. Proper synchronization of time across the network is essential for timed key rotation to function correctly. Using protocols like NTP ensures that all routers maintain a consistent time reference, which is a prerequisite for managing key lifetimes accurately.

EIGRP authentication helps prevent various types of network attacks. One common threat is the introduction of a rogue router, which may send falsified routing updates in an attempt to attract or disrupt traffic. With authentication in place, such a router would be unable to form neighbor relationships unless it possessed the correct key. Another threat involves accidental misconfiguration, where a technician might connect a router to the wrong interface or use the wrong AS number. If authentication is required and the keys do not match, the routers will not form an adjacency, preventing the misconfigured device from participating in the routing process.

When authentication fails, EIGRP provides diagnostic messages and logs that help identify the problem. Routers may log messages indicating that an authentication failure occurred due to a mismatched key or missing key. Administrators can use commands such as show ip eigrp neighbors and debug eigrp packets to observe the behavior of EIGRP on authenticated links. If the neighbor relationship is not forming as expected, these tools can reveal whether Hello packets are being received, whether the authentication field is present, and whether the key is being rejected. These insights are critical for resolving configuration issues and maintaining secure EIGRP operations.

In larger networks, especially those with multi-vendor environments or segmented routing domains, it is important to maintain documentation of key configurations and ensure that all routers within the same EIGRP domain use consistent settings. While EIGRP authentication improves security, it also increases the complexity of configuration management. A mismatch in key identifiers, key values, or key lifetimes can lead to neighbor loss and routing instability. Automated configuration management tools and centralized documentation can assist in maintaining consistency across the network.

The implementation of EIGRP authentication must also be aligned with broader security policies. For example, some organizations may mandate that all routing protocols use encrypted authentication mechanisms. In such cases, MD5 is the minimum acceptable standard, although it is worth noting that MD5 has known vulnerabilities and is not considered cryptographically strong by modern standards. In highly secure environments, EIGRP may be run in conjunction with other technologies that provide additional encryption and integrity checking, such as IPsec tunnels or control-plane policing.

Despite its age, EIGRP's authentication features remain relevant and effective when implemented properly. The protocol's reliance on shared secrets and per-interface configuration allows for detailed control and robust protection of routing exchanges. In environments where routing stability is paramount, and where untrusted devices may have physical or virtual access to the network, the use of EIGRP authentication provides an essential layer of defense.

It is also important to test EIGRP authentication in a lab environment before deploying it in production. Lab testing allows administrators to verify key synchronization, router behavior during key changes, and the impact of key expiration. It also provides a safe environment to observe how routers react to authentication failures, how they log errors, and how quickly they can recover from misconfiguration. This knowledge helps avoid outages during live deployments and ensures that authentication is not just configured, but operational and effective.

As organizations continue to place greater emphasis on securing the network infrastructure, protocols like EIGRP must be configured to resist threats, both accidental and malicious. Authentication transforms EIGRP from a trusted protocol into a secured protocol. While EIGRP on its own provides no encryption or privacy, authentication ensures that routing information comes from legitimate sources and that network integrity is preserved. In the context of modern network design, where security is no longer optional, EIGRP authentication should be considered a default requirement in any serious deployment. Through careful planning, correct implementation, and routine maintenance, EIGRP authentication becomes a reliable and valuable tool for building trustworthy and resilient routing domains.

Chapter 22: EIGRP Route Summarization

Route summarization in EIGRP is a powerful feature that allows network administrators to reduce the size of routing tables, improve routing efficiency, and limit the scope of routing updates in complex networks. Summarization refers to the process of representing multiple contiguous subnets with a single summary address. EIGRP supports manual route summarization, which gives engineers precise control over how routes are advertised. This capability is especially useful in hierarchical network designs where multiple networks can be grouped and announced as one, significantly improving scalability and simplifying troubleshooting.

EIGRP supports summarization at any point in the network because it is a classless routing protocol. Unlike classful protocols, which only summarize based on major network boundaries, EIGRP allows summarization to occur on any bit boundary, giving it the flexibility to match real-world addressing schemes more accurately. Summarization in EIGRP is performed on a per-interface basis. This means that an administrator can configure summarization on specific outbound interfaces, which allows for fine-tuned control over what summary routes are advertised and where.

To understand the benefits of EIGRP summarization, consider a router that has learned multiple routes within a contiguous block, such as 192.168.1.0/24 through 192.168.6.0/24. Without summarization, each of these routes is advertised individually to upstream routers, increasing the size of the routing table and potentially causing unnecessary route calculations during network changes. By configuring a summary route such as 192.168.0.0/21 on the outbound interface, the router can advertise a single entry that covers all the included subnets. This not only reduces the number of routes seen by adjacent routers but also helps contain the impact of route flapping or instability within the summarized block.

The configuration of EIGRP summarization involves specifying the summary route on the interface through which it should be advertised. For example, on a Cisco router, the command ip summary-address eigrp [AS-number] [summary-address] [subnet-mask] is applied directly to the interface. This instructs the router to advertise the specified summary address instead of individual routes that fall within that range. If the router detects that no more specific routes exist in its routing table to support the summary, it will stop advertising the summary as well, ensuring accuracy in route propagation.

One of the benefits of EIGRP summarization is the automatic creation of a route to null0. When a summary route is configured, the router automatically installs a route pointing the summary address to the null interface. This is a safety mechanism designed to prevent routing loops. If a router receives a packet destined for an IP address within the summarized range but for which no more specific route exists, the packet will be discarded instead of being forwarded endlessly. This technique ensures that summarization does not introduce black holes or forwarding errors in the network.

EIGRP also supports automatic summarization, which was enabled by default in older versions of Cisco IOS but is now disabled by default in modern deployments. Automatic summarization causes the router to summarize routes at classful boundaries when advertising across major network boundaries. While this feature can reduce routing table size in simple, classful networks, it can also cause reachability issues in networks with discontiguous subnets. As a result, most network designers prefer to leave automatic summarization disabled and rely exclusively on manual summarization for better control and predictability.

Proper planning is essential when implementing route summarization. The selected summary address must accurately represent the range of subnets being summarized. Summarizing too broadly can result in traffic being misrouted or dropped if some destinations within the range are unreachable. Summarizing too narrowly defeats the purpose of the feature by failing to reduce the routing table effectively.

Calculating the appropriate summary address requires understanding binary subnetting and ensuring that the summary includes all desired subnets while excluding those that should not be included.

In large-scale environments, such as service provider or enterprise core networks, summarization helps reduce the amount of routing information exchanged between regions or administrative domains. Summarization boundaries can be used to limit the propagation of instability, preventing local outages from affecting the entire routing domain. This is particularly valuable in networks with multiple branches, where each branch advertises its routes as a single summary to the central office. If a specific subnet within the branch fails or flaps, the summarized route remains stable, shielding the core routers from unnecessary recalculations.

Summarization also enhances convergence performance. When a topology change occurs within a summarized block, only the internal routers within that block need to recalculate their routes. The routers beyond the summarization point remain unaffected because they only see the summary route. This isolation significantly improves the responsiveness and stability of the routing domain, especially in large and dynamic networks.

Troubleshooting summarized networks requires an understanding of how summary routes are generated and propagated. Administrators must be able to determine which subnets are included in a summary and verify that the appropriate more-specific routes exist to support the summary. Tools such as show ip route, show ip eigrp topology, and traceroute are essential for verifying route advertisement and path selection. Additionally, access to debugging tools can help identify issues where summarized routes are advertised without valid supporting routes or where reachability is lost due to overly broad summarization.

Another consideration is the interaction between route summarization and EIGRP route filtering. Summarized routes can be filtered from advertisements just like any other route. When filters are applied, it is important to ensure that the summary remains valid and that necessary routes are not inadvertently blocked. Combining summarization and filtering requires careful design to avoid introducing inconsistencies or unreachable destinations in the network.

In multi-area or hierarchical EIGRP deployments, route summarization becomes a strategic tool. At key points in the network, such as between core and distribution layers, summarization can be used to abstract the lower-level network details and present a cleaner, more scalable routing view. This abstraction reduces cognitive overhead for network administrators and allows for simpler policy application, monitoring, and documentation. It also helps with network migrations, as summarized routes provide a stable reference point while internal details are restructured or upgraded.

Ultimately, EIGRP route summarization is more than just a method for reducing the number of routes. It is a design strategy that enhances performance, stability, and scalability. When implemented with precision and aligned with a well-structured addressing plan, summarization transforms the routing infrastructure into a more efficient and manageable system. Whether applied at branch boundaries, between layers of a campus network, or across regional sites, EIGRP summarization remains a vital practice for any network engineer aiming to build a robust and responsive IP routing environment.

Chapter 23: EIGRP for IPv6

EIGRP for IPv6 is the natural extension of the Enhanced Interior Gateway Routing Protocol into the world of Internet Protocol version 6. As networks continue to adopt IPv6 for its virtually unlimited addressing space and improved efficiency, it is essential for routing protocols to support this transition seamlessly. Cisco developed EIGRP for IPv6 by maintaining the robust and efficient features of EIGRP for IPv4 while adapting the configuration model and operational behavior to align with the standards and requirements of IPv6. Though the protocol's logic remains largely the same, there are key differences in how EIGRP for IPv6 is configured and operates compared to its IPv4 counterpart.

One of the first noticeable differences with EIGRP for IPv6 is the shift from using network statements under the routing process to interface-based configuration. In EIGRP for IPv4, administrators define a routing process and then use network statements to specify which interfaces should participate in EIGRP. However, with EIGRP for IPv6, the protocol is enabled directly on each interface using interface-level commands. This change reflects the IPv6 philosophy of making interfaces the core element of configuration and control. To begin EIGRP for IPv6 configuration, the routing process is still defined, but no networks are specified. Instead, the interfaces are activated one by one.

The EIGRP for IPv6 process requires a unique router ID, just as in IPv4. The router ID is a 32-bit number that identifies the router uniquely within the EIGRP domain. This ID does not use an IPv6 address but instead follows the traditional dotted-decimal format. It can be manually configured or automatically derived from the highest loopback interface address, assuming an IPv4 address is still available. Because IPv6 does not always guarantee the presence of an IPv4 address, it is best practice to configure the router ID explicitly when deploying EIGRP for IPv6 to ensure consistent behavior and avoid unexpected results.

Once the EIGRP for IPv6 process is created and the router ID is configured, the next step is to enable the protocol on interfaces. This is done by entering the interface configuration mode and applying the appropriate command to enable EIGRP for the IPv6 autonomous system. For example, the command ipv6 eigrp [AS-number] enables EIGRP on that interface for the specified autonomous system. At this point, the router begins sending EIGRP Hello packets to discover neighbors on that link. The link-local address is used as the source and destination for these packets, which is a critical change from IPv4. All EIGRP for IPv6 neighbor relationships are formed using link-local addresses, which are only valid on the local segment. This means that each interface must have a unique and functional link-local address to participate in EIGRP for IPv6.

Because EIGRP for IPv6 uses link-local addressing for neighbor relationships, route advertisements also use these addresses as the next-hop values. This behavior requires careful interface-level troubleshooting and design, especially in environments where link-local address duplication or misconfiguration can occur. Monitoring EIGRP neighbors is still performed using the show ipv6 eigrp neighbors command, which displays the link-local address of each neighbor, the interface over which it was learned, the hold time, uptime, and other relevant statistics.

Another change in EIGRP for IPv6 is the way the routing process is activated. In EIGRP for IPv4, once the process is defined and interfaces are matched by network statements, it becomes active automatically. In contrast, EIGRP for IPv6 requires an explicit command to start the routing process using no shutdown under the routing configuration mode. This small but important detail often catches administrators off guard when first deploying EIGRP for IPv6, as the process remains inactive even after interface-level configuration until it is manually enabled.

Despite these differences, the core operational mechanics of EIGRP for IPv6 mirror those of EIGRP for IPv4. The protocol still uses the Diffusing Update Algorithm to calculate loop-free paths and maintain backup routes. It uses Hello, Update, Acknowledgment, Query, and Reply packets to manage routing information and ensure fast convergence. The metric calculation is still based on bandwidth and delay by default, with the option to include reliability and load through configurable K-values. Feasible successors are maintained in the topology table, and the feasibility condition continues to ensure loop-free backups.

Route summarization is supported in EIGRP for IPv6, but it must be configured manually at the interface level. This aligns with the overall design of IPv6, where manual control over summarization is preferred to prevent unintended route aggregation. Summarization in EIGRP for IPv6 improves scalability and reduces the number of routes advertised between areas or across different segments of the network. The null route associated with summary addresses still exists, acting as a safeguard to prevent traffic from being routed incorrectly when more specific prefixes are unavailable.

Authentication, another essential aspect of EIGRP security, is handled differently in EIGRP for IPv6. Since IPv6 was designed with integrated security in mind, EIGRP for IPv6 uses IPsec for authentication and encryption. Unlike IPv4, where authentication is configured directly within the routing protocol, EIGRP for IPv6 relies on IPv6 Security Associations and the Authentication Header to secure routing messages. This method provides stronger security and better integration with modern security policies. However, it also requires more planning and configuration effort, including the setup of key exchange mechanisms and policies.

EIGRP for IPv6 supports advanced filtering and policy routing through route maps and prefix lists, much like its IPv4 counterpart. These tools allow network administrators to control which routes are advertised, accepted, or redistributed into EIGRP. Redistribution from other routing protocols, such as OSPFv3 or static routes, is supported and behaves similarly to IPv4. The metrics must be explicitly defined during redistribution to ensure proper path selection and prevent routes from being ignored or miscalculated.

From a design perspective, deploying EIGRP for IPv6 offers the same benefits as the IPv4 version, including fast convergence, support for unequal-cost load balancing, and reduced bandwidth consumption due to its event-driven nature. These advantages make EIGRP for IPv6 an excellent choice for networks that require high performance, scalability, and flexibility. Its simplicity of configuration at the interface level and the use of link-local addresses for neighbor formation make it well-suited for both small and large deployments. However, it also demands attention to detail, especially in terms of address planning, process activation, and link-local addressing behavior.

As organizations transition to IPv6, the availability of familiar and trusted protocols like EIGRP can ease the migration process. Network administrators already familiar with EIGRP for IPv4 will find that the learning curve for IPv6 is manageable, provided they understand the architectural shifts required by the new protocol stack. By leveraging EIGRP for IPv6, network engineers can continue to use a protocol that offers speed, reliability, and deterministic behavior, all while adapting to the demands of modern IPv6-based networking environments.

Chapter 24: EIGRP Troubleshooting

Troubleshooting EIGRP requires a structured approach, a solid understanding of how the protocol operates, and familiarity with the tools and commands available on Cisco devices. EIGRP is a dynamic, intelligent routing protocol that uses the Diffusing Update Algorithm and a variety of packet types to maintain efficient and loop-free routing tables. However, when things go wrong, misconfigurations, physical connectivity issues, mismatched parameters, or faulty routing policies can disrupt routing behavior. Knowing where to look and how to interpret the protocol's behavior is essential for resolving issues quickly and restoring full network functionality.

The first step in troubleshooting EIGRP is to verify neighbor relationships. Without established neighbors, EIGRP cannot exchange routing information. The show ip eigrp neighbors command is the primary tool for examining the current neighbor table. This output provides details such as neighbor IP addresses, uptime of the adjacency, hold timers, and retransmission statistics. If no neighbors appear in the table, the issue is typically related to Layer 2 connectivity, interface configuration, or protocol mismatches. Verifying that both routers are in the same EIGRP autonomous system is critical. If two routers use different AS numbers, they will not form an adjacency, even if everything else appears to be configured correctly.

Another common cause of failed adjacencies is mismatched K-values. These values control how EIGRP calculates its composite metric, and they must be identical on both sides of the link. If one router includes load or reliability in its metric calculation and the other does not, the neighbor relationship will fail silently. Checking K-values can be done using the show running-config command, and administrators should confirm that all devices within an EIGRP domain use the same set of metric weights. Additionally, authentication settings must be consistent between peers. If one side has MD5 authentication enabled and the other does not, or if the keys do not match, EIGRP Hello packets will be rejected, and no adjacency will form.

Interface issues also commonly impact EIGRP operation. Administrators should confirm that interfaces are operational, assigned the correct IP addresses, and enabled for EIGRP participation.

The show ip interface brief and show ip protocols commands help identify which interfaces are active and which are being used by the EIGRP process. EIGRP can also be disabled on specific interfaces using passive interface configuration. If a neighbor fails to appear, checking whether the interface has been set to passive mode is important. A passive interface will advertise its network into EIGRP but will not send or receive Hello packets, preventing adjacency formation.

Once neighbors are successfully established, the next step is to verify the routing information being exchanged. The show ip eigrp topology command reveals the full EIGRP topology table, including all known paths to destinations, their associated metrics, and which routes are installed in the routing table. If expected routes are missing, administrators must determine whether the problem lies in route advertisement, reception, or filtering. Using the show ip route command confirms whether a particular destination has been installed in the routing table, while show ip protocols indicates what networks are being advertised and whether any route filters are applied.

Route filtering is a powerful feature that can also cause unintended results if misconfigured. Distribute-lists, prefix lists, and route maps can be used to control which routes are advertised or accepted by EIGRP. If routes are being learned or sent inconsistently, checking for filtering policies is essential. Misapplied distribute-lists can prevent critical subnets from being propagated, while improperly ordered prefix lists can block necessary updates. Verifying the logic and order of filters ensures that only the intended prefixes are affected. Commands such as show run | include distribute-list or show route-map can help identify and debug these issues.

Summarization and route aggregation can also introduce complications in an EIGRP network. If a router is configured to advertise a summary address, it may omit more specific routes that are still needed for certain destinations. Additionally, the automatically created null0 route associated with the summary could cause packets to be discarded if the summary includes unreachable subnets. Troubleshooting summarization issues involves confirming which routes are present in the routing table and determining whether specific destinations are covered by a valid, active route or being black-holed due to the summary's null route. Proper planning of summarization boundaries and ensuring supporting routes exist is necessary to avoid these problems.

Another layer of troubleshooting involves the performance and behavior of the EIGRP protocol itself. High CPU usage, excessive EIGRP query traffic, or constant active route states are signs of instability. When EIGRP enters the active state for a route, it indicates that no feasible successor exists and that the router is querying neighbors for a new path. If the network is poorly designed or lacks sufficient redundancy, these queries can spread widely and cause slow convergence. The show ip eigrp topology active command displays which routes are in the active state and can help identify which destinations are causing delays. Reducing query scope through summarization or the use of stub routers can improve convergence and limit the impact of topology changes.

Troubleshooting path selection is also important. When multiple paths exist to the same destination, EIGRP selects the route with the lowest feasible distance, as long as it satisfies the feasibility condition. If a backup route exists but is not selected, it may be due to the feasibility condition not being met. This condition ensures loop-free routing by requiring that the advertised distance of the backup path be lower than the feasible distance of the primary path. If no feasible successors are available, traffic will follow only the primary path until a topology change occurs. Unequal-cost load balancing can be enabled using the variance command, but it must be configured carefully to ensure suboptimal paths are not chosen.

Packet-level troubleshooting may be required when deeper investigation is needed. Enabling debugging with commands like debug eigrp packets or using packet capture tools can reveal whether Hello, Update, or Acknowledgment packets are being exchanged as expected. However, debugging should be used with caution in production environments due to its potential impact on performance. Monitoring EIGRP traffic in a lab or during maintenance windows allows administrators to analyze packet flows and pinpoint timing, authentication, or compatibility issues between devices.

Finally, logging and historical data provide additional context for understanding EIGRP behavior over time. Logs can reveal when neighbor relationships were lost or reestablished, when routes changed state, and what events triggered EIGRP recalculations. Reviewing system logs and correlating them with network events helps isolate root causes and provides insight into the stability of the routing domain. Proactive monitoring, combined with periodic audits of configuration and topology, allows network teams to identify potential issues before they lead to outages.

Troubleshooting EIGRP is both a technical and analytical process that requires knowledge of protocol mechanics and the ability to interpret system behavior. With the right tools, commands, and design practices, administrators can ensure that EIGRP functions reliably, adapts quickly to changes, and supports the performance and scalability demands of modern networks.

Chapter 25: Implementing EIGRP in Cisco

Implementing EIGRP in a Cisco environment is a straightforward yet powerful process that allows network engineers to leverage the protocol's advanced features such as rapid convergence, route summarization, support for unequal-cost load balancing, and loop-free path selection. Cisco developed EIGRP as an enhancement of the traditional distance-vector routing model, combining features of link-state protocols with the simplicity of distance-vector operation. The result is a protocol that provides high performance, scalability, and flexibility across diverse network topologies. Understanding how to properly configure, verify, and optimize EIGRP on Cisco devices is essential for building robust enterprise-grade networks.

To begin implementing EIGRP on a Cisco router, the first step is to define the routing process. This is accomplished in global configuration mode using the command router eigrp [autonomous-system-number]. The autonomous system number identifies the routing domain and must match on all routers that are expected to become neighbors. Once the process is initiated, the router is ready to begin participating in EIGRP; however, no interfaces are active within the protocol until they are explicitly defined using network statements.

The network command under the EIGRP routing process is used to specify which interfaces will participate in EIGRP. This command does not advertise the listed networks directly but instead enables EIGRP on interfaces that match the network statement. For example, using network 192.168.1.0 0.0.0.255 tells the router to activate EIGRP on any interface whose IP address falls within the 192.168.1.0/24 subnet. Wildcard masks are used instead of traditional subnet masks, allowing for flexible inclusion of multiple interfaces. Once enabled, these interfaces begin sending and receiving EIGRP Hello packets, attempting to discover and form neighbor relationships with other EIGRP routers on the same segment.

EIGRP uses Hello packets to form and maintain neighbor relationships. These packets are multicast to 224.0.0.10 and include essential information such as the autonomous system number, hold time, and K-values. For two routers to become neighbors, their AS numbers must match, their primary interfaces must be within the same subnet, and their K-values, which are used for metric calculation, must be identical. If these parameters align, an adjacency is formed, and the routers begin exchanging topology information through Update packets.

Cisco routers provide several commands to verify EIGRP operations and assist with troubleshooting. The command show ip eigrp neighbors displays all current neighbors, their IP addresses, uptime, and queue counts, which indicate whether packets are waiting to be sent. Another critical command is show ip eigrp topology, which reveals all EIGRP-learned routes, their feasible distances, advertised distances, and the successor and feasible successor paths. This information allows engineers to understand route selection and confirm whether backup paths are available in case of failure. The show ip route eigrp command filters the routing table to display only routes learned through EIGRP, providing a concise view of active routes in use.

EIGRP uses a composite metric based on bandwidth, delay, reliability, and load. By default, only bandwidth and delay are used, and the K-values for these metrics are set to one, while the others are set to zero. This provides a balance between performance and simplicity. Interfaces can be configured with custom bandwidth and delay values to influence route selection. For example, increasing the delay on a specific interface will cause EIGRP to assign it a higher metric, making it less likely to be used as the primary path. This approach is often used to control traffic flow in dual-path environments or to prioritize high-performance links.

Cisco routers also support advanced EIGRP features, such as authentication, route summarization, and unequal-cost load balancing. To enable authentication, MD5 keys are configured on interfaces using the ip authentication mode eigrp and ip authentication key-chain eigrp commands. The key-chain must be defined with at least one valid key, and all routers on the segment must use matching keys to form adjacencies. This prevents unauthorized devices from joining the routing domain and injecting false information.

Route summarization is configured at the interface level using the ip summary-address eigrp command. This allows the router to advertise a single summarized route in place of multiple specific routes, reducing routing table size and update traffic. The summarization boundary creates a null0 route for the summary address to prevent traffic black holes. Summarization is especially useful at aggregation points, such as between distribution and core layers, where multiple access-layer subnets can be represented by a single address.

Unequal-cost load balancing is another powerful feature of EIGRP that sets it apart from many other routing protocols. By default, Cisco routers perform equal-cost load balancing across paths with identical metrics. However, EIGRP can be configured to perform load balancing across paths with different metrics using the variance command. The variance value multiplies the metric of the best path by the specified factor, and any path with a metric less than or equal to this result is eligible for installation in the routing table. This allows for more efficient use of network resources and can improve redundancy and throughput.

Cisco IOS also allows for fine-tuned control of EIGRP behavior through offset lists, route maps, and distribute lists. Offset lists can artificially increase the metric of specific routes learned from or advertised to particular neighbors. Distribute lists can filter routing updates based on access lists or prefix lists, allowing administrators to control which routes are advertised or received. Route maps provide even greater control by allowing conditional modification and filtering of routing information based on a wide range of criteria.

In dual-stack environments, Cisco routers support both EIGRP for IPv4 and EIGRP for IPv6. The configuration model for EIGRPv6 is different, focusing on interface-level activation and requiring explicit router ID configuration. While the core protocol behavior remains the same, adjustments in configuration and monitoring commands reflect the underlying differences between IPv4 and IPv6 networking. Implementing EIGRPv6 on Cisco routers provides seamless support for future expansion and dual-protocol coexistence.

When EIGRP is deployed correctly in a Cisco environment, it provides a high-performance, scalable, and resilient routing solution. The combination of fast convergence, efficient use of bandwidth, and advanced features makes it ideal for modern enterprise networks. Cisco's extensive command set, configuration options, and built-in diagnostic tools allow for easy management and troubleshooting of EIGRP deployments. Network engineers must not only understand how to configure EIGRP but also how to monitor, adjust, and optimize it to meet evolving business and technical needs. With proper planning and implementation, EIGRP on Cisco devices continues to be a reliable and effective protocol for dynamic routing in diverse and demanding network environments.

Chapter 26: Implementing EIGRP in MikroTik

MikroTik routers running RouterOS offer a versatile and cost-effective platform for building dynamic networks, and although EIGRP is not natively supported in RouterOS as a built-in routing protocol, there are scenarios where engineers may simulate EIGRP environments or use interoperability features for integration. While RouterOS has robust support for routing protocols like OSPF, BGP, and RIP, it does not officially include EIGRP, which remains proprietary to Cisco. However, in networks that include both Cisco and MikroTik devices, understanding how EIGRP might be handled or integrated indirectly becomes important, especially when interoperability is required through redistribution, tunneling, or migration scenarios. In this context, implementing EIGRP in a MikroTik environment is more about supporting coexistence and leveraging features that allow it to operate within or transition to EIGRP-based domains.

In hybrid networks where EIGRP is the core protocol and MikroTik devices must participate, one of the most effective approaches is route redistribution. Since EIGRP itself cannot be configured on MikroTik routers using RouterOS, the common strategy involves redistributing EIGRP routes into another supported protocol such as OSPF or BGP. On the Cisco side, this means redistributing EIGRP into OSPF or BGP, and on the MikroTik side, enabling the matching protocol and configuring appropriate filters to manage the imported routes. For example, if a Cisco router is redistributing EIGRP into OSPF, a MikroTik router can be configured as an OSPF peer and receive the routes that originated from the EIGRP domain. This setup allows MikroTik to interact with EIGRP-learned routes even if it cannot run EIGRP directly.

To implement this, administrators on MikroTik routers must enable OSPF under the routing menu, assign router IDs, and configure areas and interfaces properly. Interface-based OSPF configuration allows for precise control over how and where routes are received. Filters such as prefix lists or routing rules can then be used to selectively accept only the desired routes that were originally part of the EIGRP domain. Using routing marks and route preferences, administrators can further refine the behavior of imported routes to prevent conflicts or suboptimal path selection. This strategy provides a clean and structured way to integrate MikroTik into larger networks that still depend heavily on EIGRP.

Another practical scenario involves the use of static routing combined with tunneling techniques. In some cases, MikroTik routers may need to exchange routes or traffic with EIGRP-enabled devices in a manner that doesn't require full routing protocol integration. GRE tunnels or IPsec VPNs can be configured between Cisco and MikroTik routers, effectively bridging different routing environments. Inside the tunnel, static routes can be assigned, or even dynamic routing can occur through supported protocols. This allows for transparent communication while respecting the limitations of protocol compatibility. GRE tunnels are particularly useful in cases where multiple routes or networks need to be delivered to MikroTik devices from EIGRP-based infrastructures.

Migration strategies are another reason to study the implementation of EIGRP-like behavior in MikroTik. As some networks transition away from proprietary protocols like EIGRP to open standards such as OSPF or BGP, MikroTik devices often play a role in the migration process. Engineers may need to build dual-routing environments temporarily, where Cisco devices continue to run EIGRP, while MikroTik devices handle the same routing information through redistributed OSPF or BGP. During this transition, close monitoring is essential to ensure consistency, prevent loops, and maintain route accuracy. Route redistribution must be done carefully with appropriate metrics and filters to preserve performance and prevent routing anomalies.

In advanced use cases, network administrators may simulate EIGRP-like behavior in MikroTik by mimicking route selection logic using policy routing and route metrics. For instance, administrators can configure static routes with different distances and preferences to create primary and backup paths. Although this does not replicate EIGRP's dynamic nature or the DUAL algorithm, it can provide similar path control in simpler topologies. By adjusting administrative distance and manually configuring failover paths, MikroTik can deliver functionality that resembles EIGRP's feasible successor mechanism, though without its full dynamic responsiveness.

Monitoring and diagnostics play a vital role in any hybrid or redistributed EIGRP implementation. MikroTik offers tools such as Torch, Packet Sniffer, and Routing Tables view to inspect traffic flows and verify that imported routes are being used correctly. Log files and SNMP-based monitoring provide visibility into changes in routing behavior, and diagnostic commands like ip route print or routing ospf route print help validate that EIGRP-learned routes redistributed into OSPF or BGP are correctly received and installed in the MikroTik routing table. This visibility is especially important when network issues arise due to mismatched metrics, route flapping, or asymmetric routing.

Security is another consideration when implementing EIGRP integration in MikroTik. Because MikroTik does not support native EIGRP authentication, administrators must rely on securing the transport layer, such as using IPsec tunnels or filtered peerings in OSPF or BGP. Cisco routers running EIGRP may use MD5 authentication, but this is not directly compatible with MikroTik. As a result, ensuring the integrity of redistributed routes becomes a priority. Firewalls, interface-level access control, and filtering rules must be applied carefully to prevent the introduction of bogus or harmful routes into the MikroTik device from the EIGRP side of the network.

In more complex networks, the use of route maps, filters, and routing policies on MikroTik becomes indispensable. These tools allow the administrator to apply granular control over the incoming and outgoing route advertisements. For example, a MikroTik router receiving EIGRP routes redistributed via BGP can be configured with a routing filter that drops certain prefixes, sets route metrics, or tags routes for further processing. This level of customization ensures that even though EIGRP cannot be run natively, the MikroTik router behaves correctly in the context of the wider EIGRP-based environment.

Ultimately, while MikroTik does not support native EIGRP configuration, it remains a powerful platform capable of participating in or transitioning out of EIGRP networks through redistribution, tunneling, and route policy. Engineers must approach the implementation with a clear understanding of protocol boundaries, routing behavior, and integration techniques. By leveraging the strengths of RouterOS and the flexibility of Cisco's EIGRP implementation, administrators can build scalable, efficient, and interoperable networks that maintain seamless routing across multi-vendor topologies. Understanding the limitations and compensating for them with proper design allows EIGRP-based networks to extend or evolve without compromising connectivity or performance when MikroTik devices are part of the architecture.

Chapter 27: BGP Concepts and Operation

The Border Gateway Protocol, or BGP, is the routing protocol that forms the backbone of the global Internet. It is responsible for inter-domain routing, meaning it is used to exchange routing information between different autonomous systems. An autonomous system is a collection of IP networks and routers under a common administration that share a unified routing policy. BGP is defined in several RFCs, with the most current standard being BGP version 4, or BGPv4. Unlike interior gateway protocols such as OSPF and EIGRP, which are designed to operate within a single organization or network, BGP is an exterior gateway protocol, intended to manage and control routing between organizations, service providers, and large-scale enterprise networks.

One of the fundamental concepts of BGP is its path-vector nature. BGP maintains a table of routes, known as the BGP routing table, and uses various attributes to determine the best path to reach a destination. Among these attributes, the AS-path is the most significant. The AS-path is a list of autonomous systems that a route has passed through, and it plays a central role in preventing routing loops. When a BGP router receives a route advertisement, it examines the AS-path. If its own AS number is already present in the path, the route is discarded to prevent loops. This loop prevention mechanism is simple yet highly effective in a vast and decentralized environment like the Internet.

BGP operates over TCP, using port 179, which ensures reliable communication between peers. Before any routing information can be exchanged, BGP routers must establish a TCP connection and form a peer relationship, known as a BGP session or BGP neighbor. BGP supports two types of peer relationships: internal BGP (iBGP) and external BGP (eBGP). iBGP sessions occur between routers within the same autonomous system, while eBGP sessions are established between routers in different autonomous systems. The behavior and requirements of these two types of sessions differ. For example, iBGP requires a full mesh of peerings between all routers unless route reflection or confederation techniques are used, while eBGP does not.

Route selection in BGP is based on a series of attributes that provide administrators with powerful tools for policy enforcement. The selection process begins by comparing the weight and local preference, which are used for internal routing decisions. If those are equal, BGP considers the AS-path length, preferring shorter paths. Next, BGP evaluates the origin attribute, giving preference to routes with an IGP origin over those with an EGP or incomplete origin. Additional attributes like MED (Multi-Exit Discriminator) and BGP communities allow even more granular control over how routes are advertised and selected. The route with the best combination of these attributes is chosen as the best path and installed in the IP routing table.

Unlike interior routing protocols that focus on finding the shortest or fastest path, BGP prioritizes policy and control. This makes BGP uniquely suited to inter-domain routing where different organizations may have complex business agreements, performance considerations, or traffic engineering goals. BGP allows administrators to implement routing policies that reflect these real-world constraints. For example, a service provider may use BGP communities to tag routes received from customers and apply routing policies based on those tags. Similarly, BGP attributes like local preference can be used to prefer one transit provider over another, even if that provider offers a longer path in terms of AS count.

One of the key operational differences in BGP compared to IGPs is its use of incremental updates. BGP does not send periodic full updates. Instead, it sends updates only when there is a change in the routing information. When a route is withdrawn or altered, only that specific change is propagated to peers. This behavior reduces bandwidth consumption and provides greater stability, especially in large networks. However, it also means that convergence can be slower, as BGP is not designed to react as quickly to link failures as IGPs. This trade-off is acceptable in inter-domain routing, where stability and predictability are more important than rapid convergence.

BGP routers store received routes in the BGP table and select the best path to each destination. This best path is then injected into the main IP routing table, also known as the RIB (Routing Information Base). BGP supports multiple path capabilities, allowing routers to keep additional routes for redundancy or traffic engineering purposes. These paths can be used in load balancing or failover scenarios, depending on the configuration of the network and the capabilities of the router.

BGP also plays a crucial role in supporting advanced network architectures such as MPLS VPNs, data center interconnects, and cloud connectivity. In MPLS VPNs, BGP is used to distribute VPN routing information between provider edge routers. This is done using MP-BGP (Multiprotocol BGP), which extends BGP to support multiple address families, including VPNv4 and VPNv6. This allows BGP to carry customer routes with associated route distinguishers and route targets, enabling scalable and secure multi-tenant networks. In data center and cloud environments, BGP is often used to advertise virtual machine networks, manage east-west and north-south traffic flows, and integrate on-premises infrastructure with public cloud providers.

Managing BGP requires careful planning and monitoring. Misconfiguration can lead to major routing issues, such as route leaks or black holes. Because BGP announcements are accepted and propagated globally, a single erroneous advertisement can affect a large portion of the Internet. Tools like prefix-lists, route-maps, and maximum-prefix settings are commonly used to limit and filter what routes are accepted or advertised. Prefix-lists define which networks are permitted, route-maps allow conditional route manipulation, and maximum-prefix limits prevent accidental route flooding. These tools are essential for protecting the network and maintaining control over routing behavior.

Operators must also be familiar with troubleshooting tools specific to BGP. Commands such as show ip bgp, show ip bgp summary, and show ip bgp neighbors provide critical insight into the state of BGP peers, the contents of the BGP table, and the status of received or advertised prefixes. Logging and SNMP can also be integrated to alert administrators to session flaps, policy mismatches, or excessive route changes. Regular audits, monitoring of AS-paths, and route validation using technologies like RPKI (Resource Public Key Infrastructure) are becoming standard practices for securing BGP in modern networks.

BGP's design reflects the realities of inter-domain routing, where control, stability, and scalability take precedence over rapid convergence. Its rich set of attributes and flexible policy mechanisms allow organizations to define routing behavior that aligns with technical and business objectives. Although more complex to configure and manage than traditional IGPs, BGP remains the protocol of choice for connecting autonomous systems, building the Internet, and powering large-scale enterprise and service provider networks around the world. Mastery of BGP concepts and operations is a critical skill for network engineers tasked with designing, operating, or securing modern routing architectures.

Chapter 28: BGP Path Attributes

BGP path attributes are fundamental elements that define how routes are selected, advertised, and interpreted in a Border Gateway Protocol environment. They provide the information necessary for routers to determine the best path among multiple available routes to a destination. Unlike interior gateway protocols that prioritize speed and simplicity in path selection, BGP relies heavily on path attributes to support policy-based routing, allowing network administrators to influence routing decisions in a highly granular and predictable way. Understanding how BGP path attributes function is critical for anyone managing inter-domain routing, especially when traffic engineering, redundancy, and business policy alignment are required across multiple autonomous systems.

The BGP decision-making process begins once multiple paths to a single prefix are received. Instead of simply choosing the shortest or fastest route, BGP evaluates a list of path attributes associated with each route. These attributes are used to determine the most appropriate route based on specific criteria. Some attributes are well-known and mandatory, meaning all BGP implementations must understand and use them, while others are optional and may be either transitive or non-transitive. Transitive attributes are passed along even if a router does not understand them, while non-transitive ones are discarded if not recognized. Each attribute carries a specific role in shaping the behavior of BGP and the resulting forwarding decisions.

One of the most important BGP path attributes is the AS-path. This attribute lists the autonomous systems that a route has traversed on its way to the local router. The AS-path serves two key purposes. First, it provides loop prevention by allowing routers to detect if a route has already passed through their own AS. If a router sees its own AS number in the AS-path, it rejects the route to avoid creating a loop. Second, the AS-path length is used as a tiebreaker during route selection. Shorter AS-paths are preferred because they represent routes that have passed through fewer autonomous systems, and are therefore generally assumed to be more direct.

Another critical attribute is the NEXT_HOP, which indicates the IP address that should be used to reach the advertised route. In eBGP, the NEXT_HOP is typically the IP address of the router that sent the advertisement. In iBGP, the NEXT_HOP remains unchanged unless the advertising router is also a route reflector or a redistribution point. This behavior requires special attention in iBGP environments because the NEXT_HOP might not be directly reachable without proper IGP configuration. Ensuring reachability to the NEXT_HOP is essential for the successful installation of BGP routes into the routing table. Routers often use the IGP to verify that the NEXT_HOP address is resolvable before considering a BGP route valid.

The LOCAL_PREF attribute is a well-known discretionary attribute used within an autonomous system to indicate the preferred exit point for outbound traffic. The higher the LOCAL_PREF value, the more preferred the path. Unlike AS-path, which is mostly used between autonomous systems, LOCAL_PREF is applied internally and helps influence the direction of traffic leaving the AS. For example, if an organization has two exit points to the Internet and prefers one over the other, it can assign a higher LOCAL_PREF to routes learned from the preferred exit. This ensures that all routers in the AS choose the same exit path, creating consistency and predictable routing behavior.

The MED, or Multi-Exit Discriminator, is an optional non-transitive attribute used to influence inbound traffic from neighboring autonomous systems. It tells external peers which entry point into the local AS is preferred. A lower MED value is more attractive. MED is typically used between two or more autonomous systems that have multiple interconnection points. It allows the AS receiving the routes to make a more informed decision about where to send incoming traffic. Since MED is not transitive, it is not passed beyond the first neighboring AS. This limits its influence and confines its use to adjacent AS relationships.

Weight is another path attribute that plays a role in Cisco BGP implementations. It is a proprietary attribute used only within a single router and is not propagated to other routers. The primary purpose of the weight attribute is to give local preference for route selection. Routes with higher weight are preferred, and it is often used for influencing outbound traffic from a specific router. For instance, if a router receives two routes to the same destination, one via eBGP and one via iBGP, assigning a higher weight to the eBGP route ensures it is selected, even if other attributes are equal. Because weight is not shared, it offers localized control without impacting the rest of the AS.

The ORIGIN attribute indicates how the route was introduced into BGP. There are three possible origin types: IGP, EGP, and INCOMPLETE. Routes with IGP origin were generated by a network statement in BGP and are preferred over EGP or INCOMPLETE routes. EGP routes are extremely rare today and refer to routes learned through the now obsolete Exterior Gateway Protocol. INCOMPLETE origin indicates that the route was redistributed from another routing protocol into BGP. The ORIGIN attribute is used as a tiebreaker in path selection and helps routers distinguish between different sources of routing information.

BGP communities are optional transitive attributes that allow tagging of routes with information that can be used for policy decisions. Communities are numerical values that can be assigned to routes and then matched in route maps or policy statements. For example, a provider may tag customer routes with a specific community to indicate service level or preferred treatment. BGP supports standard and extended communities, and large-scale providers often define their own community-based routing policies. This mechanism allows for scalable and flexible control of route behavior, especially in multi-tenant or service provider environments.

The ATTRIBUTES themselves form the foundation of BGP's path selection process. When multiple routes to a destination exist, the BGP best path selection algorithm uses the attributes in a specific sequence to determine which path is preferred. The order includes evaluating weight, local preference, originated routes, AS-path length, origin type, MED, eBGP over iBGP, and finally metrics such as IGP cost to the NEXT_HOP. This structured approach ensures deterministic and consistent route selection across all BGP routers within an AS.

Advanced features such as route reflection, confederation, and multipath routing also rely on proper understanding and manipulation of BGP path attributes. These attributes give operators the tools they need to implement highly customized and scalable routing policies. Whether optimizing for performance, cost, redundancy, or compliance with service-level agreements, path attributes offer the knobs that make BGP one of the most flexible routing protocols in existence.

By mastering BGP path attributes, network engineers gain the ability to shape traffic flows precisely, avoid routing loops, balance loads, and influence inter-domain routing with confidence. Each attribute plays a specific role in the broader operation of BGP, and knowing when and how to apply them effectively is essential for operating modern, multi-domain, and multi-provider networks. As the Internet and enterprise networks continue to evolve, the strategic use of BGP path attributes remains at the heart of scalable and policy-driven routing architecture.

Chapter 29: BGP Neighbor Establishment

The establishment of neighbor relationships is the foundational process in BGP that enables routers in different autonomous systems, or within the same autonomous system, to exchange routing information. Unlike interior gateway protocols such as OSPF or EIGRP, where neighbor relationships are automatically discovered through multicast Hello packets, BGP requires manual configuration of neighbor relationships. This explicit and deliberate configuration is one of the protocol's distinguishing characteristics, reflecting its focus on security, policy enforcement, and control. Establishing a BGP session, also known as a peering or neighbor adjacency, involves multiple phases and requires a solid understanding of TCP, configuration parameters, and the different rules that apply to internal and external BGP sessions.

BGP uses the Transmission Control Protocol as its transport mechanism, specifically operating over TCP port 179. Because of this, BGP inherits the reliability of TCP for guaranteed delivery, flow control, and session management. Before any routing information is exchanged, a TCP connection must be established between the BGP-speaking routers. Once TCP is active and stable, BGP moves to establish a session by exchanging OPEN messages. These messages contain essential information such as the router's BGP version, AS number, hold time, BGP identifier (typically an IP address), and optional capabilities such as route refresh or support for additional address families.

There are two types of BGP neighbor relationships: External BGP, or eBGP, and Internal BGP, or iBGP. An eBGP session is formed between routers in different autonomous systems and is commonly used between service providers or between an enterprise and its Internet provider. An iBGP session is formed between routers in the same autonomous system and is used to distribute BGP-learned routes throughout the AS. Although both types of sessions use the same message types and session establishment process, their behavior and requirements differ significantly. For example, eBGP peers must typically be directly connected unless the TTL is adjusted to support multi-hop sessions, whereas iBGP peers can be multiple hops away and often require a full mesh or the implementation of route reflection to scale.

The process of establishing a BGP neighbor relationship follows a well-defined finite state machine. BGP goes through several states: Idle, Connect, Active, OpenSent, OpenConfirm, and Established. In the Idle state, BGP is waiting for a configuration or administrative trigger to initiate a connection. In the Connect state, BGP attempts to establish a TCP session. If successful, it transitions to the OpenSent state and sends an OPEN message. If unsuccessful, it may transition to the Active state, where it repeatedly tries to initiate a connection. Once both peers exchange OPEN messages, BGP enters the OpenConfirm state, during which KEEPALIVE messages are exchanged. When each router receives a valid KEEPALIVE message from its peer, the session transitions to the Established state. Only in the Established state can UPDATE messages be exchanged, meaning routing information is shared and processed.

BGP uses several timers to control the session and maintain its stability. The most important of these are the Keepalive timer and the Hold timer. The Keepalive timer defines how often BGP routers send KEEPALIVE messages to maintain the session. The Hold timer specifies how long a router will wait without receiving a KEEPALIVE, UPDATE, or NOTIFICATION message before declaring the session down. These timers must be negotiated during the OPEN message exchange and must be compatible for the session to function properly. By default, most routers set the Hold timer to 180 seconds and the Keepalive timer to 60 seconds. Adjusting these timers can impact convergence speed and stability.

Successful BGP neighbor establishment depends on several factors. Both routers must be configured with the correct neighbor IP address and autonomous system number. Mismatched AS numbers will prevent the formation of an adjacency. In the case of eBGP, the AS number configured for the neighbor must match the remote AS, while in iBGP the local and remote AS must be the same. Additionally, the BGP version must be compatible. While most modern routers use version 4, which is backward compatible, it is still important to confirm that both peers support the necessary capabilities. Misconfigured BGP identifiers or capabilities can also prevent a session from reaching the Established state.

Authentication is another feature that can affect neighbor establishment. BGP supports MD5 authentication, which requires both routers to have matching keys configured. If one router expects authentication and the other does not provide it, or if the keys differ, the TCP session will fail to establish. Authentication enhances security by ensuring that only trusted peers can establish a BGP session, protecting against unauthorized route injection and session hijacking. When authentication is enabled, debugging tools and logs become essential for verifying proper key configuration and for troubleshooting failed sessions.

Route policies and prefix filters do not affect the establishment of a BGP session, but they do influence what routes are accepted and advertised once the session is up. However, access control lists, firewall rules, or interface settings can impact whether the initial TCP session is allowed. Ensuring that TCP port 179 is open and reachable between the two routers is a prerequisite for successful BGP peering. In complex network environments or across administrative domains, path MTU, TCP MSS, and other transport-level parameters may also affect the session and should be examined during troubleshooting.

Verifying a BGP session requires the use of specific commands, depending on the router vendor. On Cisco routers, show ip bgp summary provides a snapshot of BGP peer states, uptime, the number of prefixes received, and any errors encountered during session establishment. The command show ip bgp neighbors offers detailed information about the capabilities negotiated, timers in use, and message statistics. On MikroTik, Juniper, and other platforms, similar commands exist under their respective routing menu structures. Consistent monitoring of BGP sessions, combined with logging and SNMP alerts, helps ensure ongoing stability and quick detection of problems.

In large-scale networks, managing BGP neighbors can become complex. Solutions like route reflectors and BGP confederations are used to reduce the number of peerings required in iBGP environments. Route reflectors allow a single router to redistribute routes learned from one iBGP peer to others, eliminating the need for a full mesh. Confederations divide a large AS into smaller sub-ASes, reducing complexity while maintaining the appearance of a single AS to external peers. These design enhancements do not change the core BGP neighbor establishment process but do alter how sessions are structured and maintained.

The establishment of BGP neighbor relationships is a critical step in building scalable, policy-driven, and globally connected networks. It requires precision in configuration, a deep understanding of TCP/IP mechanics, and attention to the operational distinctions between internal and external BGP. Whether peering across the Internet or within a large enterprise, the success of BGP depends on stable and correctly configured neighbor sessions. As routing tables grow and interconnectivity increases, maintaining robust and secure BGP peerings becomes more important than ever in ensuring the resilience and performance of global network infrastructure.

Chapter 30: BGP Route Selection Process

The BGP route selection process is a fundamental mechanism that allows routers to determine the best path among multiple available routes to a given destination. Unlike interior routing protocols that focus primarily on the shortest or fastest path, BGP is designed to make routing decisions based on policies and attributes. These policies may reflect administrative preference, contractual agreements, performance goals, or security considerations. Because BGP is responsible for managing routing between autonomous systems on the global Internet, its route selection process must be both deterministic and highly flexible. BGP evaluates a series of attributes in a specific order, and this sequence is critical to understanding how routes are chosen and how network behavior can be influenced.

When a BGP router receives multiple route advertisements for the same prefix, it does not immediately install all of them into the routing table. Instead, it stores them in the BGP table and begins evaluating them using a strict order of selection rules. The goal is to choose a single best path to install in the routing information base. The first attribute evaluated is the highest weight. Weight is a Cisco-specific, local attribute that is not propagated to other routers. It is used to influence route selection locally on a single router. If one path has a higher weight than the others, it is selected immediately without further comparison.

If the weight is the same across all paths, the next attribute considered is local preference. Local preference is a well-known discretionary attribute used within a single autonomous system to indicate which exit point is preferred for outbound traffic. The higher the local preference value, the more preferred the path. Unlike weight, local preference is propagated to all internal BGP routers within the AS. This makes it a powerful tool for enforcing routing policies across the entire organization. Local preference can be set using route maps or policy statements and is commonly used to prefer one ISP over another for outbound traffic.

If local preference is equal, BGP then checks whether the route was originated by the local router. Routes that are originated locally, either through the network command or redistribution, are preferred over those learned from other routers. This preference ensures that routers prioritize their own directly originated routes over those received from peers, even if all other attributes match. This behavior is particularly useful in environments where multiple routers advertise the same prefix but one of them is the actual originator.

The next attribute in the decision-making process is the shortest AS-path. The AS-path records the sequence of autonomous systems a route has traversed. BGP prefers routes with a shorter AS-path because they are typically more direct. This rule plays a vital role in interdomain routing where multiple external paths are available. Network administrators often use AS-path prepending to manipulate this decision by artificially lengthening the AS-path to make a route less desirable to peers. This technique helps control inbound traffic by influencing how other networks select their best path.

If the AS-path lengths are identical, BGP examines the origin attribute. This attribute describes how the route was introduced into BGP. The three possible values are IGP, EGP, and INCOMPLETE. Routes with an origin of IGP are preferred over EGP, and EGP is preferred over INCOMPLETE. The IGP origin typically results from the use of the BGP network command, EGP is rarely seen today, and INCOMPLETE usually results from route redistribution. This step is useful as a tiebreaker when multiple routes have identical AS-paths and previous attributes do not yield a clear winner.

The Multi-Exit Discriminator, or MED, is then evaluated if the previous attributes are equal. MED is used to convey to external peers the preferred entry point into an autonomous system. A lower MED value is preferred. MED is only compared between routes received from the same neighboring AS. If routes come from different external autonomous systems, MED is typically ignored unless the configuration explicitly allows comparison. MED is often used between cooperating ASes or multiple links between the same AS to suggest preferred entry points for inbound traffic.

In cases where MEDs are equal or not considered, BGP prefers external BGP routes over internal BGP routes. This preference helps reduce routing loops and ensures that routes learned from outside the AS are used when available, rather than relying solely on iBGP-learned paths.

This rule also reflects the assumption that eBGP routes are more accurate representations of external topology than iBGP paths, which are redistributed internally.

If all previous attributes are still equal, the router selects the path with the lowest IGP metric to the BGP NEXT_HOP. This step means the router prefers the path where the next-hop IP address is closest in terms of internal cost. This is the first stage of the route selection process that involves the IGP, such as OSPF or EIGRP. This ensures that even if multiple BGP paths are considered equal, the one with the more efficient local forwarding path is selected. This rule connects the BGP decision-making process with the underlying internal routing infrastructure.

If the IGP metrics are also equal, the router looks at the BGP router IDs. The route with the lowest router ID is preferred. The router ID is typically the highest IP address on a loopback interface or manually configured by the administrator. This step serves as a deterministic tiebreaker when all other attributes fail to produce a winner. In rare cases where the router IDs are also equal, BGP may fall back to choosing the lowest neighbor IP address to finalize the selection.

This route selection process highlights BGP's focus on control and predictability over speed. Each attribute in the evaluation chain allows for specific policy implementation, making BGP suitable for environments where routing decisions must align with business logic, service agreements, or traffic engineering goals. By manipulating path attributes such as local preference, MED, and AS-path, network operators can effectively shape traffic flow in and out of their autonomous systems. These tools provide granular control that is essential in complex, multi-vendor, multi-provider environments.

Understanding the BGP route selection process is not only important for configuring efficient routing policies but also critical for troubleshooting. When unexpected routing behavior occurs, examining the attributes of all available routes helps identify why a particular path was chosen. Tools such as show ip bgp, show ip bgp neighbors, and show ip route provide visibility into the decision-making process and expose the values of each attribute used in comparison. Armed with this knowledge, administrators can fine-tune their configurations, optimize performance, and ensure the network behaves in line with design objectives.

As networks grow in size and complexity, the BGP route selection process remains one of the most vital elements in maintaining global connectivity. Whether applied to small enterprise networks or large-scale service provider backbones, the principles that guide BGP route selection continue to be the foundation for stable, scalable, and policy-driven routing infrastructure. Every decision made within BGP is deliberate and traceable, and mastering the intricacies of this selection process is essential for any engineer working at the core of Internet or inter-domain routing.

Chapter 31: BGP Route Filtering and Policies

BGP route filtering and policies are essential mechanisms that allow administrators to control which routes are advertised, accepted, or installed in the routing table. Unlike interior gateway protocols that operate within a trusted environment, BGP operates across administrative boundaries and over the global Internet, where routing policies must reflect business relationships, security concerns, and operational goals. In BGP, the ability to manipulate routes based on attributes and match criteria provides an unmatched level of control over traffic flow. Without careful filtering and policy design, a network can become vulnerable to route leaks, hijacks, suboptimal routing, and unnecessary traffic congestion.

Route filtering in BGP can occur in several stages and directions. Routes can be filtered inbound, meaning they are blocked or modified when received from a neighbor, or outbound, meaning the filtering applies to routes before they are sent to a neighbor. Filtering on the inbound side is typically used to protect the local network from receiving unwanted or harmful routes, such as excessively specific prefixes, reserved address spaces, or incorrect advertisements. Outbound filtering is used to control which prefixes the local AS advertises to its neighbors, often based on commercial agreements or routing optimization strategies.

Prefix lists are one of the most common tools used in BGP filtering. A prefix list allows the administrator to match routes based on network addresses and subnet masks. It supports exact matches as well as range-based filtering using le (less than or equal to) and ge (greater than or equal to) modifiers. For example, an administrator may allow only prefixes from a customer that are between /16 and /24 in length, discarding anything more specific to reduce the risk of route table bloat. Prefix lists are preferred for basic filtering because they are efficient and easy to read, making them ideal for straightforward route acceptance or denial.

Access lists can also be used in BGP filtering, although they are more commonly associated with packet filtering in firewall configurations. In the context of BGP, access lists can match routes based on prefix and are sometimes used in legacy networks or in conjunction with route maps. However, access lists lack the flexibility of prefix lists in terms of mask range filtering, which limits their usefulness in complex environments. Most modern configurations use prefix lists exclusively for route prefix matching and reserve access lists for traffic filtering at the interface level.

Route maps are a powerful and flexible tool that go far beyond simple filtering. A route map is essentially a set of conditions and actions that are applied to routes. It can match routes based on prefix lists, AS-paths, next-hop addresses, BGP communities, and other attributes. It can then apply actions such as setting local preference, modifying the MED, changing the next hop, tagging routes, or denying them altogether. Route maps are processed sequentially and can contain multiple entries with permit or deny actions. This sequential processing allows administrators to build very detailed and conditional policies, which is critical in large-scale networks or multi-provider environments.

One of the most commonly used match conditions in route maps is the AS-path. An AS-path access list can match routes based on the sequence of autonomous systems that they have traversed. This is especially useful for identifying transit routes, customer routes, or upstream provider routes. For example, a provider may create a policy to deny any route that has passed through a known blacklisted AS or may prefer routes from direct peers over those received from upstream providers. AS-path filtering is also used to implement traffic engineering strategies such as AS-path prepending, which artificially lengthens the AS-path to make a route less desirable for certain neighbors.

BGP communities are another critical component of routing policies. A community is a tag that can be attached to a route and used for grouping and policy enforcement. Communities can be well-known, such as NO_EXPORT or NO_ADVERTISE, or custom-defined. The NO_EXPORT community prevents a route from being advertised outside the local AS or confederation, while NO_ADVERTISE suppresses advertisement to any peer. Custom communities are often used by service providers to indicate the origin of a route, apply routing preferences, or signal service levels. Route maps can match on communities and set actions accordingly, such as assigning different local preferences to influence outbound routing or applying specific filtering rules.

Policy implementation in BGP must be carefully designed to ensure consistency and prevent unintended consequences. Misconfigured filters can result in the loss of important prefixes, black holes in the routing table, or excessive route advertisements. For example, failing to filter overly specific prefixes from a peer can lead to route table overload and memory exhaustion on older devices. Similarly, advertising internal routes to external peers without proper filtering can expose the network to attacks or accidental reachability. Policies must also be applied symmetrically when needed, especially in redundant environments, to maintain consistent routing behavior across multiple paths.

In enterprise environments, BGP policies are often used to control routing between branch sites, data centers, and cloud providers. Administrators might prefer traffic to use specific service providers for critical applications or avoid certain routes due to cost or latency concerns. In service provider networks, BGP policies govern how customer prefixes are received, propagated, and exported to the Internet. Providers implement extensive filtering to protect their infrastructure and enforce service-level agreements. Communities, local preference settings, and prefix filtering are all used in concert to ensure that customer routes are handled correctly and that routing decisions reflect contractual terms.

Route filtering and policy control are also essential in mitigating routing threats. BGP route leaks, where one AS unintentionally or maliciously advertises routes it should not, can disrupt global connectivity. Proper use of maximum prefix limits, strict inbound filtering, and validation through Resource Public Key Infrastructure (RPKI) can reduce the risk of such incidents. RPKI provides a way to cryptographically verify that an AS is authorized to advertise a specific prefix, adding a layer of trust to route filtering policies.

Monitoring and validation are critical in ensuring that BGP policies are functioning as intended. Network operators use tools such as route monitoring platforms, real-time alerting, and periodic audits to detect anomalies in route advertisements. Commands like show ip bgp, show ip bgp neighbors, and show route-map help verify policy application and identify unexpected behavior. Logging and SNMP integration further assist in tracking policy effectiveness and identifying policy violations before they cause significant issues.

BGP route filtering and policies provide the foundation for scalable, secure, and predictable inter-domain routing. By combining prefix lists, AS-path filters, route maps, and communities, administrators can implement highly tailored routing decisions that reflect business needs and technical requirements. The flexibility and power of BGP policy mechanisms make it the protocol of choice for networks that demand precision and control over routing behavior, whether in a small enterprise network or across the vast infrastructure of the global Internet.

Chapter 32: BGP Aggregation and Summarization

BGP aggregation and summarization are essential techniques used in modern networking to manage the size and complexity of routing tables, improve scalability, and enhance the efficiency of route propagation. These techniques help network operators reduce the number of prefixes advertised into BGP, which in turn limits the overall size of the global routing table and minimizes the amount of routing information that routers must process and store. Aggregation in BGP is particularly important in service provider environments and large enterprise networks where hundreds or thousands of individual prefixes might otherwise overwhelm the routing infrastructure.

Aggregation in BGP refers to the process of combining several more specific routes into a single, broader summary route. When a router advertises this summary, it effectively represents the collection of smaller prefixes under a single prefix that encompasses them all. For example, instead of advertising four individual /24 networks, a router might advertise a single /22 route if all four networks fall within the same contiguous range. This approach significantly reduces the number of prefixes carried across the BGP infrastructure, lowers memory and CPU usage, and contributes to a more stable and predictable routing environment.

Unlike some interior routing protocols where summarization may occur automatically at network boundaries, BGP summarization is always a manual process. It must be explicitly configured by the network administrator, which provides flexibility but also places responsibility on the engineer to ensure that summarization is applied correctly. Improper summarization can lead to black holes, where traffic is forwarded toward a summarized route but no more specific route exists on the receiving router, resulting in dropped packets. To mitigate this, BGP automatically creates a route to nullo when a summary is advertised. This null route serves as a safeguard to ensure that traffic matching the summary but not any more specific prefixes will be discarded rather than routed incorrectly.

In Cisco BGP implementations, summarization is configured using the aggregate-address command under the BGP routing process. This command specifies the summary route to be advertised and includes options to control how the summary behaves. For example, the summary-only keyword tells the router to advertise only the summary route and suppress the more specific prefixes. This is useful for keeping the routing table small and clean. Without the summary-only option, both the summary and specific routes are advertised, which may be useful in situations where fallback or route optimization is needed.

BGP summarization introduces a new path attribute known as the atomic aggregate. This attribute signals to receiving routers that the summary was created from multiple more-specific routes and that some information about the individual prefixes has been lost in the aggregation process. It informs other routers not to de-aggregate the summary unless they have more detailed knowledge of the original prefixes. Alongside the atomic aggregate attribute, BGP may also attach an aggregator attribute, which identifies the router and autonomous system that performed the summarization. These attributes are informational but help with route tracing and troubleshooting in complex networks.

When implementing summarization in BGP, it is essential to ensure that the summarizing router has visibility into all the component routes that fall under the summary. If a summary is advertised without having the corresponding specific routes in the BGP or routing table, traffic may be routed toward a destination that the router cannot actually reach. This situation is particularly dangerous in service provider networks, where incorrect summarization could affect multiple customers and result in wide-scale routing issues. For this reason, summarization is usually applied at network edges or at strategic aggregation points where the router receives and manages all component subnets.

Summarization is also widely used in the context of Internet service providers and Regional Internet Registries, which allocate IP address blocks to organizations. These blocks are expected to be aggregated whenever possible to avoid unnecessary de-aggregation in the global BGP table. A well-aggregated routing table helps preserve router resources and contributes to the stability of the global Internet. Organizations that advertise de-aggregated prefixes may be subject to filtering by some upstream providers, especially when the prefixes fall within larger known aggregates. Summarizing routes before advertising them to peers and transit providers not only keeps the routing table smaller but also helps maintain policy compliance with upstream filtering rules.

In addition to static summarization using the aggregate-address command, route maps and policy-based filtering can also be used to manipulate summarization behavior. Route maps allow administrators to apply conditions to summary advertisements, set attributes like local preference or MED, and control which peers receive summaries. These mechanisms are often used in multi-homed environments or when different summaries need to be advertised to different neighbors. For example, a provider may advertise a broader summary to one upstream peer while advertising more-specific prefixes to another for traffic engineering purposes.

BGP also supports the concept of suppressing specific prefixes within the summarization process using the suppress-map feature. This allows fine-grained control over which routes are suppressed in favor of the summary and which are advertised alongside it. This is particularly useful in cases where certain specific prefixes must remain visible to some neighbors while the rest are hidden behind the summary. When used correctly, this approach enhances policy control while maintaining the benefits of aggregation.

The importance of BGP aggregation continues to grow as the number of devices connected to the Internet increases. Without aggregation, the global BGP routing table would rapidly become unmanageable, placing significant strain on routers, consuming bandwidth for updates, and reducing convergence performance. Many best practices in BGP network design, such as hierarchical addressing, careful IP allocation, and controlled redistribution, are geared toward enabling effective summarization. These practices not only simplify route advertisements but also improve the overall security posture by minimizing the attack surface presented by individual prefixes.

Monitoring and verifying summarization is an essential part of BGP operations. Network operators use commands such as show ip bgp, show ip route, and show ip bgp summary to validate that summaries are advertised correctly and that the null route is in place. Tools like BGP looking glasses and route monitoring services allow external verification to ensure that upstream peers and transit providers are receiving the correct summaries. In large networks, route monitoring systems may also track the number of prefixes advertised to each peer to ensure that summarization policies remain consistent and that no unintentional de-aggregation occurs.

BGP aggregation and summarization are not merely optional optimization strategies but fundamental elements of scalable and maintainable routing design. When used effectively, they reduce complexity, improve performance, and reinforce operational stability. The manual nature of BGP summarization gives engineers full control over route advertisement, allowing them to align technical configurations with business policies and service agreements. As networks continue to grow in size and sophistication, the ability to implement clean, strategic summarization becomes a defining skill for network architects and BGP operators alike.

Chapter 33: BGP Confederations and Route Reflectors

As networks scale and the number of internal BGP routers increases, the need for scalable iBGP designs becomes critical. By default, iBGP requires a full mesh of peering between all BGP routers within an autonomous system to ensure complete route propagation. This requirement is necessary because iBGP does not advertise routes learned from one iBGP peer to another iBGP peer to avoid routing loops. While this rule serves an important purpose, it creates significant scalability challenges in large networks where the number of iBGP sessions grows exponentially with the number of routers. To address this limitation, BGP provides two solutions that improve scalability without sacrificing correctness: route reflectors and confederations.

Route reflectors are one of the most commonly used mechanisms to reduce the number of iBGP peerings in large networks. The core concept behind route reflection is that a designated router, known as a route reflector, can redistribute routes learned from one iBGP peer to other iBGP peers. This breaks the requirement for a full mesh by introducing a hierarchical structure where some routers act as central points for route distribution. The routers that peer with the route reflector are called clients, and the reflector itself also maintains iBGP peerings with non-client peers if needed. Route reflectors simplify the topology and reduce the total number of BGP sessions, which is particularly valuable in large enterprise or service provider networks.

When a route reflector receives a route from an iBGP client, it reflects the route to other clients and to non-client peers. When it receives a route from a non-client peer, it reflects the route to all of its clients. This behavior ensures that route propagation is preserved throughout the autonomous system while avoiding the full-mesh requirement. The use of cluster IDs allows route reflectors to prevent loops in the route reflection topology. Each route reflector adds its cluster ID to the cluster list of the BGP update, and if a router sees its own cluster ID in the cluster list of a received route, it discards the route to prevent a loop.

Route reflectors can be deployed in various topologies, including single route reflector, multiple route reflectors, and hierarchical route reflectors. The single route reflector model is the simplest but introduces a single point of failure. To increase redundancy, multiple route reflectors are deployed with overlapping client sets or peering between reflectors. In large-scale networks, hierarchical reflection is used where regional reflectors forward routes to central reflectors, allowing for even greater scalability. However, with added complexity comes the need for careful planning. Poor route reflector placement can result in suboptimal routing paths or incomplete route propagation, so it is important to analyze traffic patterns and connectivity when designing the route reflector topology.

BGP confederations are another approach to managing large-scale iBGP deployments. Confederations divide a single autonomous system into multiple sub-autonomous systems, each of which operates as a separate BGP domain internally but presents itself to external peers as a unified AS. This segmentation helps reduce the iBGP mesh requirement by limiting full mesh peerings to within each sub-AS. Routers in different sub-ASes communicate using eBGP-like sessions even though they are technically within the same administrative domain. These eBGP-like sessions follow standard eBGP behavior, including next-hop modification and AS-path prepending, which allows for more flexible route control.

Within each sub-AS of a confederation, routers use iBGP to exchange routes. Between sub-ASes, routes are exchanged using eBGP rules, but with some exceptions. For example, BGP routes within a confederation are tagged with confederation-specific AS numbers, which are stripped before the routes are advertised to external peers. This maintains the appearance of a single AS from the outside while providing the internal scalability benefits of segmentation. Confederations are particularly useful in very large service provider environments or when multiple operational teams manage different regions of a large autonomous system.

One of the key advantages of confederations is policy flexibility. Since sub-ASes use eBGP to communicate, administrators can apply routing policies, manipulate attributes like MED and local preference, and influence path selection in ways that are not possible with iBGP. This allows for more granular control over routing behavior and makes it easier to isolate and troubleshoot specific regions of the network. Confederations also allow for administrative boundaries, enabling different teams or business units to operate somewhat independently while still being part of a unified routing system.

Despite their advantages, confederations introduce some complexity. Configuration errors between sub-ASes can lead to routing inconsistencies, and the design must ensure that routes are propagated correctly across sub-AS boundaries. Monitoring and troubleshooting tools must be aware of confederation-specific behavior, and engineers must take care when configuring AS-path filters and policies, as confederation AS numbers may appear in path attributes internally but not externally. Additionally, care must be taken when redistributing routes between sub-ASes to avoid unintended routing loops or advertisement of internal routes to external peers.

In practice, many networks use a combination of route reflectors and confederations to achieve maximum scalability. Route reflectors are typically easier to deploy and manage, making them the preferred solution in most medium to large networks. Confederations are reserved for the largest networks or those with specific administrative or policy requirements. Both mechanisms solve the same fundamental problem: the need to scale iBGP beyond what a full mesh allows. When implemented correctly, they enable organizations to build large, efficient, and maintainable BGP networks that support a wide range of services and routing policies.

As BGP continues to be the cornerstone of inter-domain routing, the ability to design and manage scalable iBGP infrastructures is crucial for network engineers. Route reflectors and confederations provide the tools necessary to meet this challenge. They reduce operational overhead, simplify configurations, and support advanced routing designs. However, they also require careful planning, thorough documentation, and ongoing monitoring to ensure that the benefits of scalability do not come at the cost of routing complexity or instability. Mastery of these concepts allows engineers to build robust and adaptable networks capable of growing with the demands of modern Internet and enterprise environments.

Chapter 34: BGP Communities and Local Preference

In BGP, communities and local preference are two critical path attributes that allow network administrators to influence routing behavior within and across autonomous systems. These attributes provide powerful tools for implementing routing policies, managing traffic flows, and reflecting business relationships in the technical routing decisions made by routers. While BGP is inherently a policy-driven protocol, the use of communities and local preference allows for flexible and scalable control that can be adapted to a wide variety of network topologies and operational requirements.

The BGP community attribute is a way of tagging routes with metadata that can be interpreted by routers according to predefined or custom policies. A BGP community is a 32-bit value, typically expressed in the format of two 16-bit integers separated by a colon. This notation makes it easy to represent a community as a combination of an autonomous system number and a community identifier. For example, a route tagged with the community 65001:100 might represent a route originating from AS 65001 that should receive a specific type of treatment within the network. Communities are transitive, which means they can be passed from one BGP peer to another, allowing for coordination of routing policies across multiple autonomous systems.

There are well-known communities defined by the BGP standard, such as NO_EXPORT, NO_ADVERTISE, and NO_EXPORT_SUBCONFED. These communities have specific meanings and are recognized by all BGP-speaking routers. NO_EXPORT indicates that a route should not be advertised outside of the local autonomous system or confederation. NO_ADVERTISE means the route should not be advertised to any BGP peer, internal or external. NO_EXPORT_SUBCONFED prevents advertisement beyond the boundaries of the sub-autonomous system in a BGP confederation. These well-known communities provide a convenient mechanism for controlling route propagation without the need for complex filters or route maps.

In addition to well-known communities, network operators often define custom communities that reflect internal policies or customer requirements. These custom communities can be used to mark routes for specific handling, such as preferring certain exit points, limiting advertisement to specific peers, or applying particular quality-of-service policies. Service providers frequently publish a list of supported communities that customers can use to influence how their routes are treated. For example, a provider might support a community that indicates low latency treatment or one that signals routes should only be advertised to specific upstream providers.

The power of communities lies in their flexibility and scalability. By tagging routes with specific communities, an operator can apply policies across many routes simultaneously. Instead of configuring individual filters for each prefix, a router can match on the community attribute and apply the desired action. This approach simplifies configuration, reduces the likelihood of errors, and enables more dynamic policy changes. Communities are especially useful in large networks with many customers or peerings, where consistent route handling is essential.

To apply or interpret communities, routers use route maps. A route map can match on the community attribute and then apply actions such as modifying local preference, setting the MED, changing the next hop, or filtering the route. Route maps can also be used to assign communities to routes based on other attributes, such as prefix, AS path, or peer relationship. This bidirectional use of communities—both as match criteria and as tags applied to routes—gives operators a full toolkit for building detailed and effective routing policies.

Local preference is another key BGP attribute that determines how routes are selected within a single autonomous system. It is a well-known discretionary attribute, meaning it is propagated among iBGP peers but not to external eBGP peers. The local preference attribute is used to control outbound traffic by influencing which exit point is preferred when multiple routes to the same destination exist. The route with the highest local preference value is chosen. Unlike AS path length or MED, which are evaluated later in the BGP best path selection process, local preference is considered early, making it a strong and decisive factor in route selection.

Local preference is particularly useful in networks that are multi-homed to different service providers or connected to multiple upstream routers. For example, an organization with connections to two ISPs might prefer to send all outbound traffic for a particular destination through one ISP while using the other as a backup. By assigning a higher local preference to routes learned from the preferred ISP, routers across the network will consistently select that path for forwarding traffic. This approach allows centralized control over routing behavior without the need to configure individual routers manually.

Administrators can set local preference values using route maps, which can match on various attributes, including communities. This interaction between communities and local preference enables even more advanced policy implementation. For example, a service provider might receive routes from a customer tagged with different communities indicating primary and backup preferences. The provider can then use route maps to assign corresponding local preference values, ensuring that traffic exits the network according to the customer's intent.

Because local preference is an internal attribute, it does not affect how other autonomous systems view the route. This makes it ideal for internal traffic engineering, where operators want to control outbound traffic flow without influencing inbound traffic or affecting routing beyond their own network. It also ensures that policy decisions remain confidential, as local preference values are not visible to external peers.

When configuring local preference, it is important to maintain consistency across the network. Because local preference is propagated via iBGP, routers must be part of a functioning iBGP mesh or use route reflectors to ensure proper distribution of policy. Inconsistent application of local preference values can lead to asymmetric routing, suboptimal paths, or routing loops. Therefore, it is essential to validate policies, monitor routing behavior, and document configurations thoroughly.

Monitoring tools and BGP command outputs such as show ip bgp, show ip bgp neighbors, and show route-map are essential for verifying how communities and local preference values are being applied. These tools help administrators ensure that routes are being selected and propagated as expected and provide visibility into potential misconfigurations. Logging, SNMP traps, and route analytics platforms also contribute to proactive monitoring and rapid troubleshooting.

BGP communities and local preference represent some of the most powerful elements in the BGP policy framework. Their proper use enables networks to scale, adapt to changing business needs, and maintain optimal performance. By mastering these attributes, network engineers can implement sophisticated routing behaviors that go beyond basic connectivity and support strategic goals such as cost optimization, SLA enforcement, and security. In complex inter-domain environments, the ability to control routing through communities and local preference is essential for delivering reliable and predictable service, whether in enterprise networks, service provider backbones, or the global Internet.

Chapter 35: BGP Troubleshooting Tools

Troubleshooting BGP requires a deep understanding of its operational behavior, message types, and decision-making logic. As one of the most critical components of inter-domain routing, BGP's health directly impacts network reachability, path selection, and traffic engineering. Unlike interior routing protocols, BGP is influenced by policies, attributes, and filters that are often unique to each network. Therefore, diagnosing BGP issues involves not only confirming the technical status of the protocol but also verifying that policy configurations align with intended routing behavior. Fortunately, BGP provides a wide range of troubleshooting tools and commands that allow network administrators to gain visibility into the protocol's operation and identify the root cause of issues with precision.

One of the most basic yet powerful tools for BGP troubleshooting is the command that displays the BGP summary. On Cisco routers, the show ip bgp summary command gives a concise view of all established BGP sessions, including peer IP addresses, autonomous system numbers, uptime, the number of prefixes received from each neighbor, and the session state. If a session is in an idle, active, or connect state rather than established, it indicates a problem with neighbor configuration, TCP connectivity, or route filtering. This command is the first place most engineers go to check whether BGP peering is up and stable.

For more detailed insight into the behavior of a specific neighbor, the show ip bgp neighbors command provides comprehensive information about the capabilities negotiated, the session timers, the prefixes received and sent, and statistics about message types such as updates, keepalives, and notifications. It also lists the BGP attributes applied to received routes and gives information on any route filters or route maps in effect. If a peer is sending no routes, or routes are not being accepted, this command helps identify whether the issue is related to filtering, attribute mismatch, or session instability.

The BGP routing table itself can be explored using the show ip bgp command. This command displays all routes known to the BGP process, including those that are received from peers and the selected best paths. Each entry lists the network prefix, the path attributes, and the next hop information. This is essential for understanding how BGP is selecting routes and which paths are being preferred. By examining the AS path, local preference, MED, and origin code, engineers can validate whether the correct route was selected according to policy. If the expected route is missing or marked as not best, it often indicates a mismatch in one or more attributes that must be corrected.

When routes are not appearing in the main IP routing table, the command show ip route can help determine whether the BGP-learned route was installed. If a route is present in the BGP table but absent from the routing table, the issue might be due to administrative distance, more specific competing routes, or problems resolving the BGP next hop. This is a common issue, particularly in iBGP, where the next hop is not automatically updated unless configured or redistributed. The show ip cef command can also be used to trace how the forwarding plane is handling a specific prefix and whether it is pointing to a valid next hop.

Another key tool in BGP troubleshooting is route maps. The command show route-map displays all configured route maps, their sequence numbers, and match/set conditions. Route maps are often used to manipulate attributes like local preference, MED, or communities. Misconfigured route maps are a common source of routing anomalies, such as preferred paths not being selected or routes being denied unintentionally. Route maps can be complex and hierarchical, so carefully analyzing each line and the logic flow is important when evaluating their effect.

Prefix lists and AS-path access lists are frequently used for filtering routes in and out of BGP. The show ip prefix-list and show ip as-path access-list commands display these lists and help determine whether prefixes are being correctly matched or filtered. In situations where a router is receiving fewer prefixes than expected or is not advertising routes to peers, checking these filters is a necessary step. Filters should be updated with care, as a small misconfiguration can result in major reachability issues.

Debugging BGP messages directly is sometimes necessary during advanced troubleshooting. The debug ip bgp command and its variants allow engineers to observe BGP message exchanges in real time. This includes updates, withdrawals, keepalives, and notifications. Debug output can reveal misconfigured attributes, unexpected route advertisements, or even authentication mismatches. Because debug output can be verbose and CPU-intensive, it should be used selectively and preferably in maintenance windows or lab environments.

For analyzing BGP behavior over time, logging and SNMP traps can provide historical data. BGP session flaps, prefix count changes, and unexpected notifications can be logged and correlated with other network events. Integration with monitoring systems such as NetFlow, BGP monitoring protocol (BMP), and route analytics platforms can give a broader view of routing dynamics and help detect anomalies that are not immediately obvious from CLI outputs. These tools are especially valuable in service provider environments where BGP policies change frequently and rapid detection of errors is critical.

BGP communities and extended communities are another area where troubleshooting tools can help. The show ip bgp community command allows for verification of community tags on specific routes. This is useful when route selection or redistribution is controlled by communities and when different policies are applied based on these tags. Understanding whether a route is tagged correctly according to the intended policy can clarify why certain routing behavior is occurring, especially in complex policy-based environments.

When dealing with route convergence or performance issues, it is also useful to examine the BGP timers and update intervals. The show ip bgp neighbors command provides information about keepalive and hold times, which affect session stability. Adjusting these timers can improve responsiveness but must be done with caution to avoid flapping. Additionally, the dampening feature in BGP, which suppresses routes that flap too frequently, can sometimes cause routes to be suppressed even when they are stable again. Using the show ip bgp dampening command helps determine if a route has been suppressed due to instability and allows for verification of penalty scores and suppression thresholds.

Finally, tools like traceroute and ping should not be overlooked in BGP troubleshooting. While these are not BGP-specific, they help verify reachability between BGP peers and to next-hop addresses. If BGP sessions are not forming, or if routes point to unreachable next hops, traceroute can reveal where the failure occurs. Ping tests can confirm connectivity and latency. In cases where GRE tunnels, IPsec, or VRFs are involved, ensuring proper path and reachability at the network layer is essential before even attempting to establish BGP sessions.

BGP troubleshooting requires methodical investigation, knowledge of path attributes, and familiarity with command-line tools. Whether diagnosing session failures, incorrect path selection, or unexpected route advertisements, the combination of show commands, debug tools, filters, and monitoring systems provides a comprehensive toolkit. Skilled network engineers learn to interpret this data effectively, understanding both the technical and policy-driven aspects of BGP. Mastery of these tools not only ensures faster resolution of problems but also leads to better design, improved resilience, and more predictable network behavior in even the most complex routing environments.

Chapter 36: Implementing BGP in Cisco

Implementing BGP in Cisco environments is a process that requires attention to detail, understanding of BGP fundamentals, and careful configuration of session parameters and policies. As a protocol primarily used for routing between autonomous systems, BGP plays a crucial role in enterprise networks that are multi-homed to different Internet providers, service provider backbones, and large-scale data centers. Cisco IOS provides extensive support for BGP, offering robust tools and configuration options to control route advertisement, path selection, and peer relationships. The process of configuring BGP in Cisco routers typically begins with establishing the routing process and peering relationships and proceeds to route advertisement, policy control, and optimization.

To begin configuring BGP on a Cisco router, the administrator must first define the BGP process and assign the appropriate autonomous system number. This is done using the router bgp [AS-number] command in global configuration mode. The AS number identifies the routing domain and must match between routers that are part of the same internal BGP system. For eBGP peers, each router will have a different AS number, reflecting their membership in separate autonomous systems. Once the BGP process is active, the next step is to configure neighbors using the neighbor [IP-address] remote-as [AS-number] command. This explicitly defines the IP address of the peer and the AS it belongs to. Unlike protocols that discover neighbors dynamically, BGP requires manual configuration of all peerings.

After defining neighbor relationships, the router can begin exchanging BGP messages with its peers. These include OPEN, KEEPALIVE, UPDATE, and NOTIFICATION messages. Cisco routers automatically initiate a TCP session over port 179 to the specified peer. If the connection succeeds and the BGP parameters match, the neighbor relationship moves to the established state. At this point, the routers can begin exchanging routing information. Administrators can verify session status using the show ip bgp summary command, which lists the status of all BGP peers, including session state, uptime, and prefix count.

For BGP to advertise routes, the relevant prefixes must be injected into the BGP table. This is commonly done using the network command under the BGP routing process. The network statement instructs the router to originate a specific route, provided that the prefix is already present in the routing table from another source, such as a static route or an IGP. The network must match exactly, including subnet mask, for the router to advertise it in BGP. For example, to advertise 192.168.10.0/24, the network must be in the routing table with the exact /24 mask. If it is not, the BGP process will ignore the network command.

An alternative method of injecting routes into BGP is through redistribution. This approach involves importing routes from an IGP such as OSPF or EIGRP into BGP using the redistribute command. Redistribution must be used carefully to avoid routing loops and uncontrolled propagation of internal routes. When redistributing routes, it is important to apply route maps or prefix filters to limit which routes are advertised and to set appropriate BGP attributes, such as metrics, local preference, or communities. Without proper control, redistribution can result in the advertisement of unstable or unnecessary routes to external peers.

Cisco routers support extensive route filtering capabilities in BGP. Prefix lists, route maps, and AS-path access lists can be used to control which routes are received or advertised. For example, a prefix list can allow only specific networks to be advertised to a particular peer, while a route map can set or match various BGP attributes based on policy. The ip prefix-list and route-map commands provide the foundation for these filters, and the neighbor configuration mode is used to apply them to individual peers using the neighbor [IP-address] route-map [map-name] in|out syntax. These tools are critical for maintaining clean and controlled BGP advertisements.

Cisco also supports BGP attributes like local preference and MED, which influence routing decisions. Local preference is used within an autonomous system to prefer one path over another for outbound traffic. It is configured using route maps and is applied to incoming routes. MED is used to influence how other autonomous systems select inbound paths and is usually applied to outbound routes. These attributes must be configured consistently and verified using the show ip bgp and show ip bgp neighbors commands to ensure that they are having the desired effect.

When working with internal BGP, or iBGP, Cisco routers require a full mesh of peerings between all BGP routers unless route reflectors or confederations are used. This ensures that routing information is propagated throughout the autonomous system. Route reflectors can reduce the number of iBGP sessions needed by allowing a designated router to redistribute routes between its clients. Cisco supports route reflection through the neighbor [IP-address] route-reflector-client command. In larger networks, confederations may also be implemented to divide a single AS into multiple sub-ASes, improving scalability and administrative control.

In multi-homed environments, Cisco routers can be configured to implement path selection policies based on AS-path, prefix, community, or other BGP attributes. This enables an organization to prefer one ISP over another for certain traffic or to load-balance outbound traffic across multiple providers. Communities are frequently used for this purpose, with Cisco routers supporting both standard and extended community attributes. These tags are applied using route maps and matched to apply various policies, such as suppressing advertisements to certain peers or preferring specific exit points.

Monitoring and troubleshooting BGP on Cisco routers is supported by a comprehensive set of show and debug commands. The show ip bgp command provides a detailed view of all routes in the BGP table, including path attributes, next hop, and route origin. The show ip bgp neighbors command gives in-depth information about each peer, including received and advertised prefixes, session statistics, and policy information. When troubleshooting session establishment or routing issues, debug ip bgp can be enabled to view real-time BGP message exchanges. Cisco also supports logging of BGP events and integration with SNMP-based monitoring tools for ongoing management.

Implementing BGP in Cisco environments requires not only technical configuration but also strategic planning. IP address allocation, AS numbering, route summarization, and failover behavior must all be considered during design. BGP timers, including keepalive and hold timers, can be adjusted to control session sensitivity. Maximum prefix limits should be set on external peers to prevent route table overload from misconfigured neighbors. Additionally, the bgp dampening feature can be enabled to reduce the impact of route flapping by suppressing unstable routes until they stabilize.

Cisco provides support for advanced BGP features such as multiprotocol BGP, which allows for the exchange of IPv6, VPNv4, and multicast routing information using the same BGP session. This is configured using address-family configuration mode under the BGP process. The address-family keyword defines which protocol family is being configured, and subsequent commands allow for separate policies, filters, and route maps to be applied. This flexibility supports modern architectures such as MPLS VPNs and dual-stack IPv4/IPv6 deployments.

By mastering BGP implementation on Cisco platforms, network engineers gain the ability to build robust, policy-driven, and scalable routing infrastructures. The combination of precise configuration, rich feature support, and powerful troubleshooting tools makes Cisco routers a preferred choice for enterprise and provider networks running BGP. Whether connecting to the global Internet, exchanging routes with business partners, or managing complex internal topologies, Cisco's BGP implementation offers the functionality and control necessary to meet the demands of modern routing environments.

Chapter 37: Implementing BGP in Juniper

Implementing BGP in Juniper networks follows a distinct approach compared to Cisco due to Juniper's commitment to a clean and modular configuration structure. Juniper devices use Junos OS, a powerful and structured operating system that separates the routing engine from the forwarding engine, and organizes configuration hierarchically. In Junos, BGP is configured under the routing-options and protocols hierarchy, and policies are explicitly applied to control route import and export behavior. This policy-driven model is at the heart of Junos routing philosophy and is especially important when working with BGP, a protocol that inherently relies on policy for route control and selection.

To begin configuring BGP on a Juniper router, the administrator first sets the autonomous system number under the routing-options stanza using the autonomous-system command. This defines the local AS for the router, which will be used in all BGP communications. The next step is to define the BGP group under the protocols section. In Junos, BGP peers are grouped into logical collections known as BGP groups. Each group can be either internal or external, depending on whether the peers belong to the same AS. This distinction automatically determines whether the BGP session will behave as iBGP or eBGP. Inside each group, the administrator specifies the peer IP address using the neighbor command, along with optional parameters like authentication, hold time, and local address.

Juniper's design philosophy requires that all route advertisements and acceptances be controlled by explicit policy. By default, no routes are advertised or accepted in BGP unless an import or export policy is configured. This is a key difference from other platforms where BGP might advertise connected or statically configured networks by default. In Junos, policy statements must be created under the policy-options hierarchy and then applied using the import and export statements under the BGP group configuration. These policies control which routes are received from or advertised to a peer, as well as which BGP attributes are applied or modified.

To originate a route in BGP, Juniper requires the route to exist in the routing table. Typically, this means that the route must come from a static route, connected interface, or an IGP such as OSPF or IS-IS. To advertise that route in BGP, a policy statement must be created that matches the desired prefix and allows it to be exported to the BGP peer. For example, a policy named EXPORT-BGP might match 10.1.0.0/16 and include a then accept action. This policy is then applied to the BGP group using the export EXPORT-BGP command. If the policy is missing or misconfigured, the router will not advertise any routes, even if they exist in the routing table.

The concept of route filters is central to Junos policy. Filters can be created to match specific prefixes, prefix lengths, route types, BGP communities, AS paths, and other attributes. The term structure allows for sequential evaluation of match conditions and corresponding actions. Terms can include multiple match conditions such as prefix-list, protocol type, or next-hop, and each term can be followed by actions like accept, reject, add community, or set local preference. This granular control enables precise route management and supports advanced policy architectures. Filters must be meticulously designed and thoroughly tested, as a single misconfigured term can lead to unintended route suppression or advertisement.

Juniper provides excellent tools for monitoring and verifying BGP configuration and operation. The show bgp summary command displays all active BGP sessions, their status, peer AS, uptime, and prefix counts. This output is similar in function to Cisco's BGP summary command and is typically the first tool used to verify session establishment. For detailed information about a specific peer, show bgp neighbor [address] provides statistics about received and advertised routes, negotiated capabilities, session timers, and authentication parameters. To explore the actual BGP table, show route protocol bgp shows all BGP-learned routes and includes information such as preference, next hop, AS path, and communities.

Route preference in Junos is another concept that differs from Cisco. Junos assigns a numerical preference to each route, with lower numbers being more preferred. By default, BGP routes have a preference of 170, while IGP routes have a lower preference such as 10 or 18 depending on the protocol. This preference system determines which route is selected when multiple protocols advertise the same prefix. Within BGP, the selection process still follows standard BGP rules, evaluating attributes such as local preference, AS path, origin, MED, and router ID. The policy structure in Junos allows for explicit modification of these attributes through policy actions, enabling traffic engineering and routing optimization.

Juniper also supports BGP communities and extended communities, which can be matched and set using policy terms. Communities can be used to group prefixes and apply policy based on their tags. For example, a term might match all routes with the community 65000:100 and set a higher local preference to influence outbound routing. Community support is critical in multi-provider environments and is commonly used to coordinate traffic engineering across administrative boundaries. The show route community command helps verify community tags on received and advertised routes.

Multiprotocol BGP is fully supported in Junos, allowing for the exchange of IPv6 routes, VPNv4, and other address families. This is configured using the family clause under the BGP group. For instance, to enable IPv6 routing, the administrator adds family inet6 unicast under the group or neighbor stanza. Juniper supports routing instances and virtual routing and forwarding (VRF) tables that isolate routing domains. Each instance can run its own BGP process, allowing for full support of MPLS VPN architectures. BGP within a routing instance behaves similarly to the default instance but is logically separated from the main routing table.

Authentication in Juniper BGP is configured using MD5 hashing. This is done by defining the authentication key using authentication-key and enabling it under the BGP neighbor configuration. Both sides of the BGP session must have matching keys, or the session will not establish. Authentication helps secure the session and prevent spoofed BGP messages from forming unauthorized peerings or injecting invalid routes.

For troubleshooting, Junos offers extensive debugging and logging tools. The monitor traffic command can be used for packet-level inspection, while monitor start allows for logging of BGP events. The show log messages command displays recent system events, including BGP session changes. The traceoptions feature enables detailed protocol debugging and can be customized per protocol with specific flags and output files. This is valuable for diagnosing complex issues such as route reflection problems, flapping sessions, or unexpected policy behavior.

Implementing BGP in Juniper networks is both powerful and flexible, offering unparalleled control over routing policy and session management. The structured configuration model, combined with robust policy tools and advanced monitoring capabilities, makes Junos an ideal platform for service providers and enterprise networks requiring fine-grained control and scalability. By mastering Juniper's approach to BGP, network engineers gain the ability to build highly reliable and policy-driven routing infrastructures that support complex inter-domain connectivity and advanced traffic engineering requirements.

Chapter 38: Implementing BGP in MikroTik

Implementing BGP in MikroTik routers involves a practical and functional approach suited to both small-scale networks and complex enterprise or service provider topologies. MikroTik's RouterOS provides a graphical interface via Winbox, as well as terminal access and web interface for configuring BGP. While RouterOS differs significantly in design and terminology from platforms like Cisco or Juniper, it fully supports BGP version 4 and includes essential features such as route filtering, prefix advertisement, peer management, and routing policies. Understanding how BGP is implemented on MikroTik devices requires familiarity with its layout, menu structure, and the way routing instances and peer relationships are managed.

The first step in setting up BGP in MikroTik is to ensure that the BGP package is installed and enabled, which is typically bundled under the routing package in standard RouterOS distributions. Once the router is ready, BGP is configured within the routing section, accessible either via Winbox or the CLI. MikroTik uses the concept of routing instances, which are created under the /routing menu. While most users operate with the default instance, MikroTik supports virtual routing tables, allowing for the creation of multiple isolated routing environments. This is particularly useful when working with VRFs or segmented customer environments in an ISP scenario.

To initiate BGP, the administrator begins by creating a BGP instance under /routing/bgp/instance. Here, parameters such as the router ID and the AS number are specified. The router ID should be a unique IPv4 address used to identify the router in BGP communication. The AS number defines the autonomous system to which the router belongs. MikroTik supports both private and public AS numbers, and it can participate in both iBGP and eBGP sessions. Once the instance is defined, the next step is to configure BGP peers.

Peers are configured under /routing/bgp/peer. Each peer entry includes the remote peer's IP address, the remote AS number, the BGP instance it belongs to, and optional parameters such as TCP MD5 authentication, update source, hold time, and multihop settings. The peer relationship in MikroTik must be explicitly defined, as there is no neighbor discovery. For iBGP sessions, the update source should typically be a loopback interface to ensure reachability even if physical links fail. For eBGP sessions, the remote IP is usually on a directly connected interface unless multihop is enabled.

Once the peer is configured and the TCP session is successfully established, MikroTik begins exchanging BGP UPDATE messages. However, by default, no routes are advertised or accepted unless explicitly configured. This behavior aligns with best practices in BGP and provides a secure baseline. Routes are advertised by creating network statements under /routing/bgp/network. This tells the router which prefixes it should originate into the BGP process. For a network to be advertised, it must already exist in the routing table, typically learned via static routes, connected interfaces, or an internal routing protocol such as OSPF.

MikroTik allows administrators to manage route advertisement and acceptance using filters. These are configured under /routing/filter and can match on prefix, BGP attributes such as AS path and community, route type, and more. Filters can apply actions such as accept, discard, set local preference, add community, or modify MED. Filters are attached to BGP peers using the in-filter and out-filter parameters, which specify what routes to accept or send for each peer. Without filters, all BGP routes are accepted by default, so defining appropriate filter rules is essential for route control and security.

MikroTik supports standard BGP attributes, including local preference, MED, weight, AS-path, and communities. Route selection follows the standard BGP decision process, starting with highest weight, followed by highest local preference, shortest AS-path, and other criteria. These attributes can be modified through routing filters to influence path selection. For example, local preference can be set higher for preferred exit routes to control outbound traffic. Similarly, routes received from less desirable providers can have their local preference lowered or MED increased to de-prioritize them.

BGP communities are also supported and used to tag routes with specific identifiers for policy enforcement. Communities can be matched and set in routing filters, allowing for more sophisticated routing logic. For instance, a route with the community 100:10 might indicate that it should only be advertised to certain peers or that it should receive a lower preference. This tagging mechanism is especially useful in provider networks or when coordinating policy between autonomous systems.

Monitoring BGP on MikroTik is straightforward. The /routing/bgp/session menu displays the status of BGP peers, including established state, uptime, prefix count, and last error. The /routing/route print command shows the active routes in the routing table, with flags indicating how each route was learned. Additional tools such as traceroute and ping are also available to verify reachability and troubleshoot connectivity issues. The /tool/sniffer and /tool/torch utilities allow administrators to inspect BGP traffic in real time and verify that TCP sessions and BGP updates are flowing as expected.

MikroTik also supports advanced BGP features such as route reflectors and multipath routing. A router can act as a route reflector by setting the route-reflector-client option on a peer, allowing for scalable iBGP designs without full mesh peering. This is useful in larger networks where reducing the number of BGP sessions is critical. Multipath routing allows for installation of multiple equal-cost BGP routes in the routing table, enabling load balancing across parallel links. This feature can be enabled via routing configuration, allowing for more efficient use of bandwidth.

For networks requiring redundancy and failover, MikroTik supports BFD (Bidirectional Forwarding Detection) for fast peer failure detection. BFD can be enabled on BGP peers to reduce convergence time in the event of a link or peer failure. This capability is particularly important in real-time environments such as VoIP or financial trading networks, where route stability and recovery speed are crucial.

Security in BGP on MikroTik includes MD5 authentication for peer sessions, route filtering to block undesired prefixes, and prefix limits to prevent memory exhaustion from large route tables. Administrators can set maximum prefix limits per peer to avoid being overwhelmed by accidental or malicious route leaks. This protects the router and ensures predictable performance even when peering with external networks.

Implementing BGP in MikroTik provides a versatile and robust platform for managing dynamic routing in both enterprise and ISP networks. With support for all core BGP features, rich filtering capabilities, and advanced monitoring tools, MikroTik allows engineers to build efficient, policy-driven, and scalable routing environments. Whether used in a small office or a national ISP backbone, MikroTik's BGP implementation gives administrators the control and flexibility needed to handle complex inter-domain routing with confidence.

Chapter 39: Interoperability Between Cisco, Juniper, and MikroTik

Interoperability between different networking platforms such as Cisco, Juniper, and MikroTik is an essential aspect of modern network design. As networks expand and organizations evolve, it becomes increasingly common to integrate equipment from multiple vendors. Whether due to mergers, acquisitions, cost optimization, or feature diversity, heterogeneous environments are a practical reality for network engineers. Ensuring smooth interoperability between devices from Cisco, Juniper, and MikroTik involves more than simply connecting cables and configuring IP addresses. It requires a thorough understanding of each vendor's configuration syntax, default behaviors, feature support, and subtle differences in protocol implementation, particularly when dealing with complex protocols such as OSPF, EIGRP, and BGP.

BGP is the most frequently used protocol in multi-vendor environments because it is designed to facilitate routing between autonomous systems, which often belong to different organizations using different hardware. Fortunately, BGP is highly standardized, and its core behavior remains consistent across platforms. However, each vendor has its own way of configuring BGP, and administrators must understand how to map functions and policies correctly between systems. For example, Cisco uses route maps and prefix lists extensively, while Juniper relies on policy statements and terms, and MikroTik uses filter rules. Despite differences in syntax, the logic is the same: match conditions and apply actions to route advertisements or receptions.

When configuring BGP between Cisco and Juniper, the initial step is to establish the peer relationship. Both vendors require the definition of remote AS numbers and neighbor IP addresses. Cisco uses the router bgp command followed by the neighbor statement, while Juniper creates BGP groups under the protocols section. One important consideration is the update-source parameter. In iBGP scenarios, the source of BGP updates is often a loopback interface. Cisco uses the update-source loopback command under the neighbor configuration, while Juniper uses local-address within the BGP group. Ensuring both sides use the same source interface and that routing to that interface is functional is vital for session establishment.

Address families such as IPv4 unicast and IPv6 unicast are handled differently as well. Cisco requires entering address-family configuration mode and activating neighbors for each family. Juniper, on the other hand, allows configuration of families directly under the BGP group or neighbor hierarchy. MikroTik simplifies this by allowing family configuration under the BGP instance. Engineers must be careful to ensure that each peer supports the necessary address family and that both sides are activated for the correct families. Failure to do so will result in no route exchange even if the BGP session is established.

Route advertisement must also be managed carefully. Cisco uses the network statement or redistribution to inject prefixes into BGP, while Juniper requires that a prefix exist in the routing table and then uses policy to export it. MikroTik, similar to Cisco, uses a network statement that references existing routes. The key here is that both sides must advertise prefixes using mechanisms that are compatible and understandable. If one side expects route policy to tag or filter certain prefixes, and the other side sends routes unfiltered, mismatched routing behavior can occur. This makes route filtering and policy control essential for achieving predictable interoperability.

Route attributes like local preference, MED, and communities behave similarly across platforms, but the way they are configured differs. Cisco typically sets local preference using route maps, Juniper uses policy actions in policy statements, and MikroTik uses filter rules. These attributes must be coordinated if consistent traffic engineering behavior is expected. For example, if a Cisco router sets a high local preference on routes from one ISP, and those routes are passed to a Juniper router without modification, the Juniper router may not reflect the same preference unless a policy is applied. Careful planning of attribute handling ensures consistent path selection regardless of vendor.

Communities are another critical area of interoperability. Standard BGP communities are supported across all three platforms, and administrators often use them to mark routes for special handling. For example, a route tagged with community 100:10 may signify low priority, and all routers should treat it accordingly. On Cisco, this is done through the set community command in route maps. On Juniper, it is set using then community add in a policy term. On MikroTik, communities are set using routing filter actions. Matching community behavior across platforms allows for synchronized routing decisions and simplifies multi-vendor policy enforcement.

Another key element of interoperability is the use of authentication. All three platforms support BGP MD5 authentication. Cisco uses neighbor password commands, Juniper uses authentication-key under the neighbor stanza, and MikroTik uses the password option under BGP peer configuration. Ensuring that MD5 keys match exactly is critical, as mismatched keys prevent session establishment and generate confusing log messages that may indicate TCP issues. Moreover, ensuring that firewall rules or filters allow TCP port 179 is fundamental for all platforms, as the BGP session depends on uninterrupted TCP communication.

Route reflector and confederation configurations are also supported across all three platforms, though implementation details vary. Cisco and Juniper both support route reflection and confederation natively, while MikroTik supports route reflection but not confederations. This must be considered when designing large-scale BGP topologies. If using MikroTik in a route reflector architecture, it can serve as a client or reflector, but must not be expected to interpret confederation-specific AS-path structures. Engineers must ensure compatibility by keeping AS path policies simple and ensuring that devices within the same iBGP mesh can interpret path attributes consistently.

Monitoring and troubleshooting tools vary between vendors. Cisco provides commands such as show ip bgp summary and show ip bgp neighbors. Juniper offers show bgp summary and show bgp neighbor. MikroTik displays BGP session state under /routing/bgp/session. Understanding how to interpret these outputs across different systems allows administrators to identify session failures, policy mismatches, or attribute issues quickly. Logging and diagnostics also differ, with Juniper offering extensive traceoptions, Cisco using debug ip bgp, and MikroTik supporting packet sniffers and log-based event tracking.

Familiarity with these tools on all platforms is critical for maintaining a healthy multi-vendor BGP environment.

When dealing with route redistribution, such as injecting OSPF routes into BGP, attention must be paid to metric translation, tag propagation, and loop prevention. Cisco uses the redistribute command with route maps, Juniper uses policy statements under protocols, and MikroTik uses the redistribution and filter sections. Redistribution strategies must be coordinated, especially when routes are passed through multiple vendor devices. Without proper controls, loops and route inconsistencies can emerge.

Interoperability between Cisco, Juniper, and MikroTik is not only possible but can be highly effective when done correctly. It requires aligning protocol configurations, ensuring compatible policies, and understanding how each platform handles routing attributes and filters. Mastery of each vendor's syntax and behavior allows for seamless communication, consistent path selection, and stable routing operations. In a world where vendor diversity is common, the ability to build and maintain interoperable BGP networks ensures flexibility, scalability, and resilience in complex network architectures.

Chapter 40: Redistribution Between OSPF, EIGRP, and BGP

Redistribution between OSPF, EIGRP, and BGP is one of the most powerful and complex operations in dynamic routing. It involves taking routes learned from one routing protocol and injecting them into another, allowing connectivity between domains that do not natively share routing information. This is essential in multi-protocol environments where different parts of a network may rely on different protocols due to legacy systems, vendor requirements, scalability strategies, or administrative boundaries. While redistribution enables route exchange and inter-domain communication, it introduces challenges such as routing loops, inconsistent metrics, route filtering, and policy enforcement that must be managed carefully.

In a typical enterprise or service provider network, OSPF might be used within a single domain to provide fast convergence and hierarchical routing, EIGRP might serve in legacy Cisco-centric segments, and BGP would handle external connectivity or multi-tenant segmentation. Redistribution is the glue that connects these domains. It is commonly implemented using route redistribution commands in Cisco IOS, route import/export policies in Juniper, and filter-based redistribution in MikroTik. Regardless of the platform, the key consideration is maintaining route integrity while preventing unnecessary route propagation or loops.

When redistributing between OSPF and EIGRP, the administrator must be aware of how each protocol calculates metrics and handles route types. EIGRP uses a composite metric based on bandwidth, delay, load, and reliability, while OSPF uses a simpler cost metric typically derived from interface bandwidth. During redistribution from OSPF into EIGRP, Cisco requires a seed metric to be defined because EIGRP has no way to compute its composite metric from an OSPF cost. Without a seed metric, the redistributed routes will not be advertised. This metric is usually defined under the redistribute command using the metric keyword, specifying bandwidth, delay, reliability, load, and MTU. Similarly, when redistributing from EIGRP into OSPF, the external route types must be considered. OSPF classifies redistributed routes as either type 1 or type 2 external routes, with type 1 routes including internal cost and type 2 routes using a fixed cost regardless of the internal topology. Choosing the appropriate type depends on the desired traffic behavior and control within the OSPF domain.

BGP adds another layer of complexity. When redistributing routes into BGP, only prefixes that exist in the IP routing table can be injected into the BGP table. This means that administrative distance and route source must be verified. Cisco routers require route maps to match and control which routes are redistributed into BGP. Attributes such as AS-path, local preference, MED, and community can be set using these route maps to ensure that the BGP routes behave correctly once advertised. In Cisco IOS, the command redistribute ospf [process-id] route-map [map-name] under the BGP process allows for granular control of OSPF-to-BGP redistribution. Without filters, all OSPF routes could be injected into BGP, which may lead to route bloat or leaking internal prefixes to external peers.

The reverse process, redistributing BGP routes into OSPF or EIGRP, must be handled with even more care. Not all BGP routes are suitable for injection into IGPs. Injecting full Internet routing tables into OSPF or EIGRP can overwhelm routers and cause instability. To avoid this, route maps or prefix lists must be applied to limit which BGP prefixes are redistributed. Common practice includes filtering based on route source, prefix length, or BGP communities. Cisco supports this with commands like distribute-list or route-map filtering under the OSPF or EIGRP process. Additionally, setting a default metric is required, as BGP does not include a metric that EIGRP or OSPF can interpret. Redistributed BGP routes are considered external and may be treated differently by OSPF or EIGRP in terms of route preference and forwarding decisions.

Loop prevention is a critical concern during redistribution. Because each protocol maintains its own view of the network, it is possible for the same route to be redistributed in both directions, leading to loops. To prevent this, administrative distance, tagging, and filtering mechanisms are used. Route tagging allows the administrator to mark redistributed routes with a specific tag, which can then be matched and denied during reverse redistribution. For instance, when redistributing OSPF into EIGRP, the routes might be tagged with a specific value. When EIGRP routes are later redistributed back into OSPF, the tag can be matched and filtered to avoid reintroducing the same prefixes.

MikroTik handles redistribution through routing filters, which are applied to the import and export rules between protocols. The /routing/filter menu allows administrators to match route attributes and apply actions such as setting metrics or rejecting prefixes. For redistribution between OSPF and BGP in MikroTik, filters must be attached to the relevant protocol instances and carefully designed to avoid unintentional advertisement of internal prefixes. Filters can match on protocol, prefix length, interface, and BGP attributes, offering flexibility similar to route maps in Cisco. While MikroTik does not support EIGRP, it can redistribute routes between supported protocols such as BGP, OSPF, and static routes.

Juniper routers use a similar approach with policy statements defined under the policy-options hierarchy. Redistribution is performed using the export and import statements under the relevant protocol, applying a named policy that matches desired routes and performs actions such as setting next-hop, preference, metric, or tags. Juniper also supports tagging routes with communities or local attributes that can be matched later during redistribution, offering a structured way to manage route flow across protocol boundaries. The show route advertising-protocol and show route receive-protocol commands help verify that redistribution is working as intended and that policies are being applied correctly.

An important operational consideration is route summarization during redistribution. Summarization helps reduce the number of prefixes exchanged and prevents unnecessary propagation of detailed internal routes. Cisco supports summarization at redistribution boundaries using the summary-address command. In Juniper, summarization can be implemented using aggregate routes with specific policies to control advertisement. MikroTik allows manual summarization by filtering and injecting aggregate static routes, then advertising them through the desired protocol. However, summarization must be used carefully, especially when overlapping prefixes exist, as it can lead to routing inconsistencies or suboptimal path selection.

Ultimately, successful redistribution between OSPF, EIGRP, and BGP depends on a thorough understanding of each protocol's metrics, behavior, and filtering capabilities. It is not a simple copy-and-paste process but requires strategic planning, meticulous policy design, and ongoing verification. Tools such as traceroute, ping, show ip route, and debug commands help verify path consistency and protocol behavior. Engineers must constantly monitor the redistributed prefixes and ensure that route propagation aligns with network design and security policies. Redistribution offers the flexibility to integrate diverse routing domains but demands discipline and precision to maintain a stable and secure network architecture.

Chapter 41: Route Filtering and Policy-Based Routing

Route filtering and policy-based routing are two essential techniques used by network administrators to control the flow of routing information and manipulate traffic paths in dynamic routing environments. These strategies are not limited to any single routing protocol but are broadly applicable across OSPF, EIGRP, BGP, and static routes. They allow for greater precision in managing how routes are learned, advertised, and used for forwarding, which is particularly important in multi-vendor, multi-domain, or security-sensitive networks. While traditional routing decisions are based purely on destination IP addresses and the lowest-cost paths determined by routing protocols, route filtering and policy-based routing introduce layers of decision-making based on business logic, source IPs, applications, interfaces, or other criteria.

Route filtering is the process of allowing or denying routing updates based on defined criteria. It is commonly used to control which routes are advertised to or accepted from a peer or neighbor. This is crucial in environments where excessive route advertisements could overwhelm routers or where certain prefixes should not be visible to external networks. Filtering can be applied inbound to prevent certain routes from being installed into the local routing table, or outbound to limit which routes are advertised to peers. On Cisco devices, filtering is often implemented using prefix lists, route maps, and distribute lists. Prefix lists are used to match IP address ranges with subnet mask precision, while route maps offer more advanced logic by allowing matches on AS paths, communities, metrics, and other attributes. Distribute lists can filter routes using access control lists but are more limited in flexibility compared to route maps.

In BGP, route filtering becomes even more critical. Since BGP can exchange large amounts of routing information and operates between autonomous systems, filtering is used to implement routing policies that align with business agreements, performance goals, and security requirements. For example, an ISP may choose to filter customer routes based on prefix length, denying overly specific prefixes such as /32s, or filter out private IP ranges that should not be advertised globally. Similarly, BGP communities can be used to tag routes, and then policies can filter or prioritize them based on these tags. On Juniper routers, policies are written using policy statements with match and then clauses, offering a highly structured and modular approach to filtering. MikroTik uses routing filters where match conditions and actions are defined in a readable interface, and filters are applied to protocols or peers directly.

Policy-based routing, or PBR, extends control beyond what dynamic routing protocols provide. Instead of relying solely on destination-based decisions, PBR enables the router to consider other fields in the packet, such as source address, source or destination port, or incoming interface. This allows for customized routing decisions that can divert traffic along specific paths for purposes like bandwidth optimization, security enforcement, service-level agreements, or multi-link utilization. In Cisco IOS, PBR is typically implemented using route maps applied to interfaces with the ip policy route-map command. The route map evaluates the packet's attributes and then sets a next-hop IP address that overrides the standard routing table decision. This approach is particularly useful in environments where traffic from certain departments, applications, or services needs to be routed differently from the rest of the network.

Policy-based routing can also be used to enforce redundancy strategies or load balancing. For instance, a router may use PBR to send all voice traffic over a high-quality MPLS link while sending bulk data transfers over a less expensive broadband connection. In some cases, administrators may use tracking and IP SLA in conjunction with PBR to make dynamic decisions based on link availability or latency. This adds a level of intelligence to routing decisions that static or traditional dynamic routing cannot achieve alone. Juniper supports similar capabilities through firewall filters and routing instances, while MikroTik provides PBR through mangle rules and routing tables, allowing for per-packet control and advanced traffic manipulation.

Despite its flexibility, policy-based routing introduces complexity. Because it bypasses the normal routing decision process, it can create troubleshooting challenges, particularly when the routing table appears correct but traffic is not flowing as expected. Engineers must ensure that PBR policies are carefully designed, documented, and tested to avoid black holes or asymmetric routing. Logging and verification tools such as Cisco's show route-map, Juniper's show policy, and MikroTik's /ip firewall mangle print help identify which rules are being matched and what actions are being taken. Consistent monitoring and policy review are critical for maintaining a predictable and efficient network.

Another important aspect of route filtering and PBR is security. Filtering helps protect the network from route leaks, prefix hijacks, and incorrect advertisements, especially in BGP environments. Policies can be used to drop prefixes that are not authorized, limit maximum prefix lengths, or block routes that do not originate from known neighbors. PBR can enforce traffic separation for sensitive applications, directing them over encrypted tunnels or through firewalls. In multi-tenant environments, PBR ensures that customer traffic is isolated and directed according to contractual requirements. These tools give administrators the ability to enforce network segmentation and security without relying solely on access control lists or firewall rules.

Integration of filtering and PBR with dynamic protocols requires careful coordination. Redistribution scenarios, such as injecting BGP routes into OSPF or EIGRP, must consider filter policies to avoid flooding the IGP with unnecessary or dangerous routes. Similarly, when routing decisions are influenced by PBR, administrators must ensure that failover mechanisms and fallback paths are in place to maintain availability. It is common practice to use PBR with tracking objects or route monitoring tools so that, if a preferred next-hop becomes unreachable, traffic can revert to default routing behavior. This combination of policy and automation ensures that the network remains resilient under varying conditions.

In high-availability environments, filtering and policy-based routing contribute to deterministic behavior and failover readiness. They allow network engineers to prepare for failures, attacks, and traffic surges by building in logic that adapts to changing conditions. Policies can prioritize critical applications, drop unwanted traffic, or route around outages. The ability to craft and enforce routing behavior through intelligent filters and policies elevates routing from a static, protocol-driven process to a dynamic, business-aligned strategy. This adaptability is vital in modern networks where uptime, performance, and security are non-negotiable requirements.

Route filtering and policy-based routing are foundational elements of network design and operation. They empower administrators to shape routing behavior to match operational objectives, enforce security boundaries, and optimize traffic flows in real time. As networks grow more complex and diverse, the ability to control and refine routing decisions through policy becomes not just a best practice but a necessity. Mastery of these tools allows network engineers to craft highly resilient, efficient, and secure routing architectures that are capable of supporting both current demands and future growth.

Chapter 42: Route Maps and Prefix Lists

Route maps and prefix lists are two of the most powerful tools available in the configuration of dynamic routing protocols. They are commonly used in Cisco networks and supported with equivalent functionality in platforms like Juniper and MikroTik, albeit with different syntax and structure. These tools provide the fine-grained control needed to implement complex routing policies, influence path selection, filter route advertisements, and enforce security or administrative boundaries. Understanding how to build and apply route maps and prefix lists effectively is essential for engineers tasked with managing scalable and reliable routing infrastructures.

A prefix list is essentially a tool used to match network prefixes based on their IP address and subnet mask. Unlike access control lists that can become unwieldy when dealing with subnet variations, prefix lists offer a more scalable and readable method of filtering routes. A prefix list evaluates routes based on their prefix and prefix length using operators such as greater than or equal to and less than or equal to. For instance, a prefix list might match any subnet within 10.0.0.0/8 with a length between /16 and /24. This kind of filtering is especially useful when an administrator wants to limit the advertisement or acceptance of very specific or very broad routes. By using prefix lists in routing configurations, engineers can block unintentional advertisements of improperly summarized or unauthorized subnets.

Prefix lists are often used in conjunction with route maps. A route map is a conditional logic structure that permits or denies route updates based on a sequence of match and set commands. Each route map has a name and consists of one or more numbered entries, which are processed in order. Within each entry, match statements define the criteria that must be met, and set statements define the actions to be taken if the match is successful. Route maps can be applied in both inbound and outbound directions, affecting how routing information is received or sent between routers.

In the context of BGP, route maps are indispensable. They can be used to modify attributes such as local preference, MED, AS-path, and community. For example, if an administrator wants to prefer one ISP over another for outbound traffic, they can apply a route map that matches routes received from the preferred ISP and sets a higher local preference. Alternatively, for inbound traffic engineering, a route map can prepend the local AS number multiple times to make a route appear less desirable. Prefix lists can be used within these route maps to ensure that only specific prefixes are matched and modified. This allows for granular control over route manipulation based on specific business or technical needs.

When implementing redistribution between routing protocols, route maps and prefix lists play a crucial role. Without filtering, redistribution can lead to the injection of excessive or inappropriate routes, potentially causing instability. For example, when redistributing BGP into OSPF, route maps can be used to match only certain prefixes and apply tags or metrics. These tags can then be used later to prevent loops or apply specific policy controls. Prefix lists ensure that only the desired range of subnets is redistributed, avoiding accidental injection of unnecessary routes into the interior routing domain.

Route maps also provide functionality for implementing policy-based routing. By applying a route map to an interface with the ip policy route-map command, an administrator can direct traffic based on source address, destination, or even Layer 4 information. This overrides the default destination-based routing decision and allows for application-aware routing, traffic segregation, or redundant link utilization. Prefix lists in this context might be used to match source addresses or destinations, ensuring that only traffic from specific subnets is subjected to alternate routing behavior.

Another practical use of route maps is in controlling route summarization. Summarized routes are often advertised to reduce the size of routing tables, but in certain scenarios, some specific routes must be retained for accuracy or control. A route map can be used to suppress specific prefixes while allowing others to be summarized. This is especially useful in BGP, where the aggregate-address command can use a suppress-map to selectively hide specific prefixes during summarization. Prefix lists again serve as the matching mechanism, identifying which routes are eligible for suppression based on their prefix and mask.

In OSPF and EIGRP, route maps are also used during redistribution and filtering. When injecting external routes into OSPF, for instance, route maps can be used to classify the routes as type 1 or type 2, assign metrics, or apply route tags for further processing. The use of prefix lists in this context ensures that only routes meeting certain criteria are accepted into the process. This helps maintain consistency and prevent loops or policy violations.

In multi-vendor environments, similar functionality exists but under different terminologies. Juniper uses policy statements and prefix lists to achieve the same effect, using terms such as match prefix-list and then accept or reject. MikroTik implements filtering using routing rules and filters that reference prefix matching and actions. Regardless of the platform, the logic remains similar: evaluate the route based on predefined criteria and take an action accordingly. Therefore, understanding route maps and prefix lists in Cisco provides a strong foundation for managing routing policy in any network.

Monitoring and troubleshooting route maps and prefix lists is essential for ensuring they function as intended. Commands such as show ip route, show ip bgp, and show route-map can help verify which prefixes are being matched and what actions are being applied. Misconfigured route maps can lead to missing routes, black holes, or routing loops, so continuous validation and clear documentation are important. Prefix list counters and logging can also be used to monitor how frequently entries are matched, providing insight into the operational impact of filters.

The power of route maps and prefix lists lies in their flexibility and control. They allow administrators to design routing behaviors that align with organizational needs, enforce security policies, and optimize traffic flow. Whether used for filtering route advertisements, implementing PBR, managing redistribution, or applying summarization policies, these tools are essential components of the routing toolkit. Their modular nature makes them easy to adapt and reuse across different scenarios, making them indispensable in both enterprise and service provider networks. Mastering their use enables precise control over dynamic routing behavior and supports the creation of resilient, scalable, and efficient network architectures.

Chapter 43: Monitoring and Logging Dynamic Routes

Monitoring and logging dynamic routes is a critical component of maintaining a healthy and predictable network. In dynamic routing environments where protocols such as OSPF, EIGRP, and BGP constantly learn, exchange, and recalculate routes, visibility into routing activity is essential for both troubleshooting and performance optimization. Network engineers need to know what routes are being learned, where they are being advertised, how they are being selected, and when they are being changed. Without this visibility, it becomes nearly impossible to diagnose routing issues, identify suboptimal paths, or enforce routing policies effectively.

Dynamic routes are those that are automatically learned through routing protocols rather than being statically configured by the administrator. Because these routes can change based on network conditions, link states, or policy modifications, they must be monitored continuously. In Cisco networks, dynamic routing information is accessible through a variety of commands, with show ip route being one of the most fundamental. This command displays the current routing table and indicates the source of each route, such as O for OSPF, D for EIGRP, or B for BGP. Each entry includes the next-hop address, administrative distance, and metric, providing insights into how and why the route was selected.

For more detailed inspection, protocol-specific commands offer deeper insights. The command show ip ospf reveals the status of OSPF processes, areas, neighbor relationships, and LSAs. Similarly, show ip eigrp topology displays the EIGRP topology table, showing feasible successors and metrics. For BGP, show ip bgp presents the BGP table, including all known paths to prefixes, their attributes, and the selected best path. These outputs are essential when determining why a particular route is or is not being installed into the routing table.

Logging plays a complementary role to real-time monitoring. While monitoring provides a snapshot of the current state, logging tracks changes over time, enabling administrators to identify trends, detect flapping routes, and investigate past incidents. Cisco routers allow logging of routing protocol events, such as neighbor up/down, route additions, or protocol-specific changes. The command debug ip routing enables real-time debugging of routing table changes, while debug ip ospf, debug ip eigrp, and debug ip bgp provide detailed logging of protocol-specific activity. Because debug output can be verbose and resource-intensive, it is typically used during maintenance windows or in lab environments, although it can be filtered and redirected to syslog servers for analysis.

Syslog is an industry-standard protocol used to collect log messages from network devices. By configuring routers and switches to send logs to a central syslog server, network administrators can maintain an archive of routing events and correlate them with other system activity. This is especially valuable for identifying the cause of network outages or performance degradation. Log messages can include timestamps, severity levels, and detailed descriptions of routing changes, making it easier to reconstruct the sequence of events leading up to a problem.

SNMP-based monitoring tools also play a vital role in tracking dynamic routing. Tools like SolarWinds, PRTG, and Nagios can be configured to poll routing tables, interface states, and protocol metrics at regular intervals. They can generate alerts when routing changes exceed a certain threshold, such as when a route flaps repeatedly or when a neighbor relationship fails. These alerts can be used to trigger incident response procedures or notify administrators of potential issues before they escalate. SNMP traps provide a more proactive mechanism, allowing devices to send immediate alerts when predefined routing events occur.

NetFlow and similar traffic analysis tools complement route monitoring by showing how traffic is actually flowing through the network. While routing tables show the intended path, NetFlow reveals the real-time behavior of traffic, which can highlight discrepancies caused by asymmetric routing, policy-based routing, or failover scenarios. Analyzing NetFlow data alongside dynamic routing logs provides a complete picture of network health and performance, enabling faster troubleshooting and better-informed network design decisions.

In Juniper networks, monitoring and logging are achieved using commands such as show route, show ospf neighbor, and show bgp summary. Junos OS also supports traceoptions, a powerful feature that allows detailed protocol debugging with fine control over what is logged and where logs are stored. Traceoptions can be configured to log only certain event types, which helps reduce noise and focus on relevant information. The logs can be written to files for long-term analysis or monitored in real time. Junos also integrates well with external monitoring platforms using syslog, SNMP, and streaming telemetry, allowing for scalable and flexible monitoring solutions.

MikroTik routers offer a variety of monitoring tools under the Winbox interface and command-line interface. The /routing route print command displays the active routing table, showing learned routes and their sources. The /routing ospf lsa print and /routing bgp advertisements commands provide protocol-specific insights. MikroTik also supports routing filters that log matches, enabling administrators to verify that filters are working correctly. Logging can be directed to local files, the system log, or remote syslog servers. MikroTik's /tool sniffer and /tool torch allow for packet-level inspection, which is especially useful when verifying BGP or OSPF packet exchanges during session establishment or troubleshooting.

For advanced environments, telemetry and automation provide real-time streaming of routing data to centralized platforms. Technologies such as gRPC, NETCONF, and RESTCONF allow routers to export routing information in near real-time to collectors and automation engines. These tools enable proactive network management, where anomalies are detected through machine learning or predefined logic and acted upon automatically. Integrating dynamic routing telemetry with other network data sources creates a holistic monitoring environment capable of detecting and responding to complex network conditions quickly and accurately.

Maintaining route stability is another critical goal of monitoring. Route flapping, where a route is repeatedly added and removed, can cause significant CPU load on routers and instability across the network. Route dampening can be configured to suppress unstable routes temporarily. Monitoring tools can detect route flaps and calculate flap counts, allowing administrators to take corrective action before they impact performance. Analyzing flap patterns can also reveal underlying issues such as unstable links, misconfigured routing protocols, or hardware failures.

Regular auditing of the routing table is also a best practice. Auditing involves comparing the actual routing table against the expected state based on design documentation. Discrepancies may indicate misconfigurations, unauthorized changes, or policy violations. Automated scripts or compliance tools can assist with this process, generating reports and alerting administrators to any deviations.

Effective monitoring and logging of dynamic routes ensure the stability, security, and performance of a network. By combining real-time command-line monitoring, automated logging, centralized collection, and intelligent alerting, network engineers can maintain visibility into every aspect of the routing infrastructure. This visibility allows for rapid detection of issues, data-driven decision-making, and proactive optimization of routing policies. Whether in enterprise networks, service provider backbones, or hybrid cloud environments, monitoring and logging of dynamic routes form the foundation of resilient and well-managed network operations.

Chapter 44: Security Considerations in Dynamic Routing

Dynamic routing plays a fundamental role in modern networks by allowing routers to exchange routing information and automatically adjust to network topology changes. However, the very nature of dynamic routing introduces a range of security challenges that can jeopardize the stability, confidentiality, and integrity of the network if not properly addressed. Routing protocols like OSPF, EIGRP, and BGP are designed to operate in cooperative environments where routers trust one another. In real-world scenarios, especially in large enterprise networks or the public Internet, that assumption does not always hold true. Attackers may exploit routing protocol vulnerabilities to perform malicious activities such as route hijacking, traffic interception, or denial-of-service attacks. To protect against these threats, network engineers must implement layered security strategies that include authentication, route filtering, traffic validation, and monitoring.

One of the most basic yet crucial security measures in dynamic routing is authentication. Most modern routing protocols support some form of authentication to verify the identity of routing peers. For example, OSPF supports plain-text and MD5 authentication, while BGP and EIGRP also support MD5. By configuring authentication on all routing sessions, administrators can ensure that only authorized devices can participate in the routing process. In OSPF, authentication is configured per interface or area and must match on both sides of the link. In BGP, each peer must use the same authentication key. This prevents rogue devices from forming neighbor relationships and injecting malicious routes into the routing table.

However, authentication alone is not sufficient to secure a routing domain. Route filtering is an essential complement to authentication. Filters control which routes are accepted, advertised, or redistributed between protocols. For instance, prefix lists and route maps in Cisco networks can be used to block private IP ranges from being advertised externally via BGP. They can also prevent the acceptance of prefixes that are too specific, which could lead to route table exhaustion or traffic redirection. In BGP environments, filtering is critical for preventing route leaks and hijacks. A route leak occurs when internal routes are accidentally or maliciously advertised to external peers, while a hijack involves announcing prefixes that belong to other organizations. Both can disrupt Internet traffic and cause outages. Proper filtering and adherence to prefix advertisement policies can mitigate these risks.

A more advanced technique to secure BGP is the implementation of the Resource Public Key Infrastructure, or RPKI. RPKI allows network operators to cryptographically sign their route announcements and validate received prefixes using Route Origin Authorizations (ROAs). Routers configured with RPKI validation can verify whether a given prefix is authorized to be announced by the AS that claims it. If the validation fails, the route can be marked as invalid and rejected. This prevents a significant class of BGP hijacking attacks and adds a layer of trust to interdomain routing. Though adoption has been growing, RPKI still faces challenges such as deployment complexity and reliance on external validators, but its role in securing global routing is increasingly recognized.

Dynamic routing also faces threats from packet manipulation and interception. Without encryption, routing updates can be observed or altered by attackers on the same network segment. This is especially relevant in environments where routers communicate over untrusted links, such as public wireless or shared provider infrastructure. To counter this, routing protocols should be deployed over encrypted channels whenever possible. Technologies like IPsec and GRE tunnels can provide secure transport for routing messages. Additionally, some routing protocols support native encryption. For example, OSPFv3 can operate over IPsec natively, offering both authentication and encryption of routing updates.

Monitoring and logging are vital for detecting and responding to routing-related threats. A well-configured network should generate alerts for anomalous behavior such as route flaps, sudden changes in the number of prefixes received, or unexpected peer relationships. These events may indicate misconfiguration or an active attack. Tools like syslog, SNMP traps, and telemetry provide real-time visibility into the state of routing protocols. Integration with Security Information and Event Management systems allows for correlation between routing events and other security incidents, enabling a faster and more informed response.

Access control is another fundamental aspect of dynamic routing security. Routers should be configured to accept routing protocol messages only from explicitly trusted peers. Access control lists can be applied to routing interfaces to limit traffic to known neighbors. On devices like MikroTik, filters and interface lists help manage which routes are processed and from which interfaces routing messages are accepted. On Cisco devices, passive interfaces can be used to disable routing protocol advertisements on certain links entirely. These measures help reduce the attack surface and limit the opportunity for unauthorized devices to influence routing behavior.

Route redistribution introduces yet another layer of complexity and potential vulnerability. Improperly configured redistribution between protocols like BGP, OSPF, and EIGRP can create routing loops, black holes, or unexpected path preferences. Route maps and tagging mechanisms should be used to control which routes are redistributed and to ensure that routes are not inadvertently advertised back into the protocol from which they originated. Tags can also be used for loop prevention in environments with complex routing architectures. Careful planning and documentation of redistribution policies are necessary to prevent security flaws from being introduced through route propagation logic.

In larger networks or service provider environments, role separation and administrative control are vital. Different teams may manage different routing domains or functions. Implementing role-based access control on network devices ensures that only authorized personnel can alter routing configurations. Configuration management systems should track all changes to routing protocol parameters, with approval workflows and audit trails to ensure accountability. This not only enhances security but also helps prevent accidental misconfigurations that could result in outages or vulnerabilities.

Security considerations in dynamic routing must also extend to hardware and software maintenance. Keeping routing devices updated with the latest firmware and software patches is critical, as many routing vulnerabilities are discovered and mitigated through vendor updates. Devices running outdated operating systems may be susceptible to known exploits that can be used to compromise routing protocols. Regular vulnerability assessments and penetration testing can help identify weaknesses in routing configurations and ensure that all best practices are being followed.

Dynamic routing, while powerful and flexible, must be deployed with a strong focus on security. From neighbor authentication and route filtering to monitoring, encryption, and access control, each layer contributes to the overall integrity and resilience of the routing infrastructure. As threats continue to evolve and the complexity of networks increases, the importance of securing dynamic routing cannot be overstated. Network engineers must approach routing not just as a technical task but as a security-critical function that demands continuous attention, testing, and improvement. The ability to secure routing protocols directly influences the availability, performance, and safety of the entire network, making it a core responsibility of every network professional.

Chapter 45: Real-World OSPF Deployment Scenarios

Open Shortest Path First, or OSPF, is one of the most widely deployed interior gateway protocols in enterprise and service provider networks. Its link-state design, hierarchical architecture, and support for multiple areas make it an ideal choice for environments that require scalability, fast convergence, and detailed routing control. In real-world scenarios, OSPF is deployed in a variety of topologies and organizational structures, each designed to meet specific performance, security, or administrative requirements. Understanding these scenarios provides valuable insight into how OSPF functions beyond theoretical configurations and highlights the flexibility and robustness of the protocol in production environments.

A common deployment of OSPF occurs in medium-sized enterprise networks where multiple buildings, departments, or data centers must be interconnected using a hierarchical design. In such cases, Area 0, the backbone area, acts as the core of the network, interconnecting other non-backbone areas. Each area is typically mapped to a specific geographic location or functional group, allowing for isolation of routing updates and improved stability. For example, Area 1 might be assigned to the finance department located in one building, while Area 2 supports the engineering team in another. Each area contains routers that only exchange link-state information within their area, and Area Border Routers, or ABRs, connect these areas to the backbone. This design minimizes LSDB flooding and SPF recalculations in areas where changes are not relevant, resulting in better performance and reliability.

In campus networks, OSPF is often deployed in a single-area configuration when the scale of the network is manageable and routing stability is the primary goal. A single-area OSPF network reduces complexity and makes troubleshooting simpler since all routers share the same LSDB. However, as the number of routers and links grows, the network may be restructured into a multi-area OSPF design to distribute the SPF calculation load and to better control the scope of routing updates. In such environments, it is important to carefully plan area boundaries and the placement of ABRs to maintain efficient routing and avoid suboptimal paths. Network engineers typically monitor the number of routes and LSA types within an area and introduce summarization at ABRs to reduce routing table size and protocol overhead.

Another common real-world scenario involves the use of OSPF in hub-and-spoke WAN topologies. In these designs, a central data center or headquarters serves as the hub, while branch offices are the spokes. Each branch might be configured in a separate OSPF area or included in a larger non-backbone area depending on administrative preference. The hub acts as the ABR, redistributing routes between the branches and Area 0. OSPF's ability to control summarization at ABRs allows the hub router to advertise a single summarized route back to each branch, reducing the routing table size and improving scalability. When redundancy is required, dual WAN links can be configured with OSPF cost manipulation to influence the primary and backup paths, ensuring that traffic takes the most efficient route under normal and failure conditions.

Stub areas and not-so-stubby areas are often deployed in networks where external route information must be controlled. In a branch office scenario where Internet connectivity is centralized at the headquarters, the branch is typically configured as a stub area to prevent the propagation of external LSAs. This reduces the number of routes the branch must process and enhances routing performance. If a branch has local Internet access or needs to inject external routes into OSPF, a not-so-stubby area, or NSSA, is configured instead. NSSAs allow the injection of Type 7 LSAs that are converted to Type 5 LSAs by the ABR and propagated into the backbone. This design balances the need for controlled route injection with the hierarchical benefits of OSPF.

In service provider networks or managed services, OSPF is used to segment customer environments through virtual routing and forwarding instances. Each VRF instance operates its own OSPF process, allowing multiple customers to coexist on the same physical infrastructure without route leakage. These OSPF instances may redistribute routes into MP-BGP or MPLS L3VPNs for inter-site connectivity. In such deployments, route redistribution is carefully controlled using route maps and filters to prevent routing loops and unauthorized route injection. The use of OSPF authentication and passive interfaces enhances security by preventing rogue routing advertisements and limiting OSPF participation to trusted links.

Datacenter environments present another real-world OSPF deployment case where fast convergence and fine-grained control are crucial. Leaf-and-spine topologies are common in modern datacenters, and OSPF can be used to provide dynamic routing between leaf switches and spine switches. Each rack or pod can be its own OSPF area or all switches can participate in a single area for simplicity. The decision often depends on the scale and desired isolation. Equal-cost multi-path, or ECMP, is leveraged heavily in these scenarios to balance traffic across multiple links, and OSPF supports ECMP natively by installing multiple equal-cost routes into the forwarding table. OSPF's rapid convergence also ensures minimal downtime during link or node failures, which is critical for latency-sensitive applications.

In merger and acquisition scenarios, OSPF plays a key role in integrating disparate networks. Often, two companies operate with different IP address schemes and routing designs. OSPF allows network engineers to segment new acquisitions into separate areas while maintaining centralized control through the backbone. Route summarization, filtering, and redistribution can be used to integrate the new network without exposing internal routing structures. Over time, the design can be refactored for better efficiency, but OSPF provides the flexibility to support both temporary and permanent integration strategies.

One more practical application is the use of OSPF over dynamic VPNs, such as those created with DMVPN or IPsec. In dynamic tunneling environments, OSPF's ability to automatically form adjacencies and exchange routes simplifies routing configuration. However, careful consideration must be given to OSPF timers and the use of unicast transport when multicast is not supported. Authentication, route filtering, and topology control are particularly important in these deployments to maintain performance and security over potentially unreliable or untrusted links.

In global enterprise networks, OSPF can be deployed in conjunction with other protocols such as BGP. OSPF handles intra-domain routing while BGP manages external connectivity. Redistribution between OSPF and BGP is common at the edge of the network and must be carefully configured to avoid loops and route propagation issues. Route tagging and filtering help prevent accidental redistribution of external routes back into the IGP. Engineers often use route maps to control what prefixes are exchanged and to enforce routing policies that reflect business requirements.

These real-world scenarios demonstrate that OSPF is not just a theoretical protocol taught in textbooks but a dynamic and adaptable tool used daily by network engineers around the world. Its ability to scale, converge quickly, and support complex topologies makes it a cornerstone of modern IP routing. By understanding how OSPF is applied in practical situations—from campus LANs and global WANs to data centers and cloud interconnects—network professionals gain the knowledge and confidence to design, deploy, and manage robust and efficient OSPF-based networks that meet the needs of today's fast-moving digital landscape.

Chapter 46: Real-World EIGRP Deployment Scenarios

Enhanced Interior Gateway Routing Protocol, or EIGRP, has long been a trusted choice for dynamic routing in Cisco-centric networks. Known for its fast convergence, loop-free operation using the Diffusing Update Algorithm, and its blend of distance vector and link-state characteristics, EIGRP has found a stable role in many real-world network deployments. Although it is not an open standard like OSPF, its efficiency and simplicity continue to make it a preferred protocol in environments where Cisco infrastructure dominates. Real-world EIGRP deployments span enterprise branch architectures, campus networks, service provider environments with MPLS edge routing, and even hybrid networks with redistribution into other protocols like BGP and OSPF. Understanding how EIGRP is deployed practically provides valuable insight into its strengths and considerations in production networks.

A classic use case for EIGRP is in enterprise branch networks that require rapid convergence, scalable summarization, and simplicity in configuration. Many organizations maintain multiple remote offices that connect back to a core data center or regional hub via MPLS, VPN, or leased lines. In these deployments, EIGRP is used to exchange routes between the hub and branch routers while leveraging automatic summarization at network boundaries to keep routing tables small. Even though automatic summarization is disabled by default in later IOS versions, manual summarization can still be applied at interfaces, providing efficient aggregation of branch subnets as they route back to the core. EIGRP's low overhead and minimal CPU requirements make it an excellent choice for branch routers that may have limited resources.

In a typical dual-hub, dual-router branch design, EIGRP is configured to provide redundancy and fast failover. Each branch office router peers with both hubs using EIGRP, and administrative distances are adjusted to prefer one hub while keeping the second as a backup. EIGRP supports unequal-cost load balancing, so if both links are active and meet feasibility conditions, traffic can be load balanced based on bandwidth or delay. This allows engineers to utilize redundant WAN paths efficiently. In the event of a failure, EIGRP quickly recalculates routes using precomputed feasible successors, often faster than OSPF's convergence process. This reliability is one reason EIGRP is heavily favored in high-availability enterprise designs.

In campus networks, EIGRP is frequently deployed in distribution and access layers due to its fast convergence and reduced configuration complexity. Unlike OSPF, which requires careful area design and LSA management, EIGRP functions without hierarchical constraints, although it still benefits from thoughtful summarization and design. Access layer switches often run EIGRP to connect to redundant distribution routers, with stub configurations enabled to reduce the amount of routing information sent to the access devices. The EIGRP stub feature prevents queries from being forwarded to these devices, improving stability and reducing CPU and memory usage. In large campus networks, this design ensures that access switches remain simple and fast while still participating in dynamic routing.

Service providers and managed service environments sometimes deploy EIGRP on the customer edge, especially when customers require a simple routing protocol to integrate with the provider's infrastructure. Even though EIGRP is Cisco proprietary, its ease of configuration and support for route filtering, route tagging, and policy-based routing make it a strong candidate for customer-premises equipment. In MPLS VPN environments, EIGRP routes are often redistributed into MP-BGP at the provider edge, allowing dynamic learning of customer prefixes while maintaining isolation and control. This redistribution must be handled with route maps or prefix lists to avoid route loops or unwanted propagation.

Another real-world scenario involves the use of EIGRP in data center interconnects or application-specific environments. In scenarios where fast convergence is essential for database replication, voice traffic, or real-time applications, EIGRP's ability to rapidly adapt to changes without needing complex tuning gives it a strong advantage. For example, in a private cloud where multiple tenant networks need to communicate with minimal downtime, EIGRP is used for east-west routing between hypervisors or virtual routers. Here, administrators take advantage of EIGRP's metric customization to prioritize specific paths or optimize performance for high-bandwidth applications. EIGRP's support for bandwidth and delay in metric calculations allows more granular control over path selection compared to protocols that rely on cost alone.

In hybrid routing environments, EIGRP is frequently used alongside OSPF or BGP, with careful redistribution controlling the exchange of routes between protocols. For instance, a network might run EIGRP internally for LAN and access routing while using OSPF for WAN connectivity or for communication with external partners. Redistribution is configured at the edge routers, typically with route maps that apply metrics, tags, and filters to avoid routing loops and ensure proper path selection. Engineers must be cautious about bidirectional redistribution, using route tagging and filtering to prevent re-advertising learned routes back into the originating protocol. This hybrid approach allows organizations to benefit from EIGRP's speed and simplicity internally while still meeting broader interoperability or policy requirements.

Security is also a key consideration in real-world EIGRP deployments. EIGRP supports MD5 authentication to verify peer identities, ensuring that only authorized devices can participate in the routing domain. Authentication is especially critical in networks that span untrusted links or customer-controlled equipment. Engineers also make use of passive interfaces to disable unnecessary neighbor formation on interfaces that do not require dynamic routing, reducing the attack surface and improving protocol efficiency. Additionally, route filtering with prefix lists and offset lists is employed to control route propagation and prevent accidental advertisement of internal subnets to the wrong areas of the network.

EIGRP is often seen in disaster recovery and business continuity designs. When organizations implement secondary data centers or failover facilities, EIGRP's fast convergence helps reduce the time required to reroute traffic during failover events. Engineers may use floating static routes in conjunction with EIGRP to prioritize primary paths while keeping backups in place and ready to activate instantly. EIGRP's ability to detect topology changes and rapidly converge makes it well suited for environments where recovery time objectives are strict and service disruptions must be minimized.

From small business networks to sprawling enterprise architectures, EIGRP continues to be a reliable and flexible protocol. Its real-world implementations demonstrate how it can be tailored to meet the needs of nearly any topology, whether through summarization, load balancing, redundancy, or hybrid redistribution. While the industry has shifted toward open standards, EIGRP's unique capabilities and straightforward operation ensure that it remains relevant and effective in modern networks. Mastery of EIGRP deployment scenarios gives network professionals the ability to design networks that are not only efficient and scalable but also highly resilient and easy to manage. Through careful planning and thoughtful application of its features, EIGRP proves itself time and again as a foundational routing solution in diverse environments.

Chapter 47: Real-World BGP Deployment Scenarios

Border Gateway Protocol, or BGP, is the cornerstone of inter-domain routing and plays a vital role in the design and operation of large-scale networks. Unlike interior routing protocols, BGP is designed to operate across autonomous systems, allowing for the exchange of routing and reachability information between different organizations, service providers, data centers, and global Internet participants. BGP's policy-based nature, scalability, and flexibility make it suitable for a wide range of deployment scenarios, each tailored to specific performance, redundancy, security, and administrative goals. Real-world BGP deployments reflect this versatility, from small enterprises with dual-homed Internet connections to global service providers with multi-tiered architectures and complex route policies.

One of the most common BGP deployment scenarios involves multihoming an enterprise network to two or more Internet Service Providers. In this configuration, an enterprise uses external BGP sessions to peer with multiple upstream ISPs, thereby achieving redundancy, load balancing, and increased reliability for Internet access. BGP allows the enterprise to announce its public IP space to both ISPs and to receive the full Internet routing table or a default route from each provider. Administrators can use local preference, AS-path prepending, and MED to influence inbound and outbound traffic flows. For example, AS-path prepending may be used to make one link appear less desirable for inbound traffic, while local preference ensures that outbound traffic prefers the primary ISP under normal conditions. This level of control provides businesses with robust failover and optimized path selection based on their specific needs.

Service providers and Internet exchange points rely heavily on BGP to manage interconnections between their customers and peer networks. A typical Internet Service Provider maintains BGP sessions with upstream transit providers, peer networks at exchange points, and downstream customers. These BGP sessions are configured with route filters, prefix lists, and community-based policies to control routing behavior and enforce service-level agreements. The ISP may offer its customers either full table routing or default routes, depending on the customer's size and routing capabilities. ISPs also use BGP communities to tag routes for specific handling, such as restricting advertisement to certain peers, adjusting local preference, or applying security policies. These community-based policies are essential for managing route propagation and ensuring that each customer receives the appropriate level of routing control.

Another significant real-world deployment involves the use of BGP within large enterprise or service provider networks to provide internal routing between various business units or geographic regions. Internal BGP, or iBGP, is used to distribute BGP-learned routes across the network without re-advertising them between internal routers. Because iBGP does not propagate routes learned from one iBGP peer to another, full mesh peering or the use of route reflectors is required. Route reflectors reduce the complexity of full-mesh peering by allowing designated routers to redistribute BGP routes to their clients. In real-world deployments, route reflectors are carefully placed to maintain redundancy and prevent single points of failure. Organizations often deploy multiple route reflectors across regions or data centers to ensure high availability and consistent routing policies throughout the network.

Data center environments frequently use BGP as the primary routing protocol due to its scalability and policy control. In modern data center designs based on spine-and-leaf topologies, BGP is used between all spine and leaf switches. This approach simplifies routing, avoids limitations imposed by spanning-tree protocols, and enables ECMP for load balancing. Each leaf switch establishes eBGP sessions with spine switches, even though they may all be under a single administrative domain. To maintain loop prevention and control propagation, the use of BGP confederations or private AS numbers with remove-private-AS configuration is common. BGP allows seamless integration of virtual routing instances, enabling multi-tenant isolation and simplified automation in cloud and hybrid environments.

In content delivery networks and distributed application environments, BGP is used to control traffic engineering and optimize latency. CDN providers deploy BGP to influence inbound traffic toward the nearest edge location based on network topology, geography, and performance. This is achieved through prefix advertisement strategies and AS-path manipulation. By announcing more specific prefixes from specific locations or using BGP communities to control advertisement scope, CDN providers can guide traffic to the optimal edge node. Additionally, BGP route health injection is used to dynamically advertise or withdraw prefixes based on server or application availability, allowing real-time adaptation to network conditions and improving user experience.

Another real-world application of BGP is in MPLS Layer 3 VPN environments, where BGP is used to distribute customer routes between provider edge routers. Multiprotocol BGP extensions enable the exchange of VPNv4 or VPNv6 routes that include route distinguishers and route targets. These attributes allow multiple customers to use overlapping IP address spaces while maintaining isolation within the provider's network. BGP policies ensure that each customer's routes are advertised only to the appropriate peers, based on route target matching. Service providers use route reflectors to scale this environment, and careful policy control is essential to prevent route leakage between VPNs. This application of BGP underpins many managed services and enterprise WAN offerings.

In disaster recovery and high-availability designs, BGP provides dynamic path control and rapid failover. Enterprises often use BGP to manage routing between primary and secondary data centers, with routing policies that shift traffic in the event of a failure. This may involve advertising specific prefixes from each site and using AS-path or MED to control traffic direction under normal operations. In the event of a failure, the affected site withdraws its prefixes, and BGP convergence reroutes traffic to the available site. When implemented properly, this mechanism ensures minimal downtime and supports critical business continuity objectives.

Security considerations in real-world BGP deployments include filtering, prefix validation, and session protection. Route filters are applied to prevent unauthorized or misconfigured prefixes from being advertised or accepted. Prefix limits protect routers from overload due to excessive route advertisements. BGP session authentication using MD5 helps prevent session hijacking, while tools such as BGP session password protection and TTL security mechanisms are used to secure the BGP control plane. In global routing environments, RPKI and BGP monitoring tools are increasingly deployed to validate the origin of advertised prefixes and detect anomalies such as route leaks or hijacks.

Across all deployment scenarios, monitoring and visibility are essential. Operators use tools like route views, looking glasses, and telemetry systems to observe BGP behavior in real time. Commands such as show ip bgp, show bgp summary, and route analytics platforms help detect issues such as flapping routes, suboptimal path selection, or unexpected changes in prefix propagation. Proper monitoring ensures that policies are being enforced as intended and enables quick response to routing anomalies or performance issues.

BGP remains the foundation of large-scale routing and continues to evolve in complexity and functionality. Its use in real-world scenarios showcases its ability to adapt to diverse requirements, whether supporting a small dual-homed office or a global multi-tier service provider network. Through thoughtful design, rigorous policy control, and ongoing monitoring, BGP enables efficient, scalable, and secure routing in the most demanding environments, ensuring reliable communication and optimized performance for organizations of every size.

Chapter 48: Performance Tuning in Large Networks

Performance tuning in large networks is a critical task that ensures efficient data transmission, minimal latency, and high network availability. As networks scale in size and complexity, the challenges of maintaining optimal performance become more pronounced. Large networks are often composed of numerous routers, switches, firewalls, and other devices, each handling significant traffic loads and routing decisions. With multiple protocols running simultaneously and diverse applications in use, the task of ensuring that network performance remains high while minimizing disruptions requires a deep understanding of the various factors that affect network operation.

One of the first considerations when tuning the performance of large networks is the design of the network architecture itself. A well-planned network topology can significantly reduce the overhead of routing protocols and minimize the distance that data must travel between devices. In large networks, hierarchical design principles are essential, as they provide a way to structure the network in such a way that traffic is efficiently routed through core, distribution, and access layers. By implementing logical segmentation through VLANs, subnets, and routing protocols like OSPF or EIGRP, network designers can localize traffic, reduce broadcast storms, and ensure that routing updates are exchanged only when necessary.

In large networks, the choice of routing protocol plays a significant role in performance. While OSPF and EIGRP are commonly used in enterprise networks, their performance can vary based on factors such as network size, topology, and the frequency of network changes. OSPF, being a link-state protocol, requires a considerable amount of overhead to maintain link-state databases (LSDBs) and to flood link-state advertisements (LSAs) throughout the network. As the network grows, OSPF's LSDB can become large, and the SPF (Shortest Path First) calculations can take longer, leading to delays in convergence. To mitigate this, network designers often break large OSPF domains into multiple areas, which helps limit the scope of LSAs and reduces the computational load on routers. The backbone area (Area 0) should always remain contiguous, and careful design of area boundaries is essential to prevent routing inefficiencies and ensure that the network converges quickly.

EIGRP, on the other hand, is a hybrid routing protocol that combines the best features of distance vector and link-state protocols. Its Diffusing Update Algorithm (DUAL) allows for rapid convergence with minimal overhead. However, even EIGRP can face performance issues in large networks, especially when the number of routes and EIGRP neighbors grows. In such cases, adjusting EIGRP timers, such as hello and hold time intervals, can help control the frequency of routing updates and improve network efficiency. Additionally, EIGRP's support for unequal-cost load balancing can be leveraged to distribute traffic more effectively across multiple paths, making the network more resilient and optimizing available bandwidth.

BGP, the de facto inter-domain routing protocol used on the Internet, is commonly deployed in large networks that require communication with external parties, such as service providers, partners, or customers. However, BGP's complexity and scale can create significant performance challenges. The global BGP routing table, for example, can contain millions of routes, which can place a significant burden on routers that must process and store this information. To improve BGP performance in large networks, administrators can configure route filtering, prefix lists, and community-based policies to limit the number of prefixes that are accepted and advertised. BGP route aggregation is another effective technique that reduces the number of routes advertised by summarizing multiple smaller prefixes into a larger, more general route. Careful use of BGP attributes like AS-path prepending and local preference can also help influence route selection and prevent suboptimal routing paths.

Another critical area of performance tuning in large networks is the optimization of multicast traffic. Multicast communication is often used for applications such as video streaming, conferencing, and real-time data distribution. In large networks, efficient multicast routing is essential to prevent excessive flooding and unnecessary bandwidth consumption. Protocols like PIM (Protocol Independent Multicast) and IGMP (Internet Group Management Protocol) play a crucial role in managing multicast traffic. Tuning these protocols by adjusting thresholds for IGMP snooping and configuring PIM on routers can help reduce unnecessary traffic, improve multicast forwarding, and optimize network resource usage.

Traffic engineering is another key aspect of performance tuning, particularly in large-scale networks with multiple paths and varying link speeds. Techniques like Quality of Service (QoS) and MPLS (Multiprotocol Label Switching) are widely used to prioritize certain types of traffic and ensure that critical applications, such as VoIP or video conferencing, receive preferential treatment. In MPLS networks, traffic can be efficiently directed along predefined paths, allowing for better utilization of network resources and avoidance of congested links. By controlling traffic flows using MPLS labels and adjusting QoS settings, network engineers can ensure that bandwidth is allocated according to the needs of the organization, improving both performance and user experience.

Another significant factor affecting the performance of large networks is the management of broadcast and multicast storms. In large LAN environments, broadcast traffic can quickly escalate and consume valuable bandwidth. Protocols like Spanning Tree Protocol (STP) can help mitigate loops and broadcast storms, but their configuration and optimization are crucial for network stability. In large networks with complex topologies, enabling rapid spanning tree protocols like RSTP or MSTP can reduce the convergence time in the event of a topology change, improving network stability and responsiveness.

Network security also plays a role in performance tuning. While security mechanisms such as firewalls, intrusion prevention systems, and encryption are critical for protecting the network, they can also introduce latency and reduce throughput if not properly configured. In large networks, the placement and configuration of security devices are crucial to ensure that they do not become bottlenecks. For example, applying security filters and policies closer to the network edge, rather than at the core, can help minimize latency and reduce the impact on internal traffic. Additionally, offloading some security functions to dedicated hardware or using techniques like deep packet inspection only when necessary can help preserve performance while maintaining strong security.

Finally, the monitoring and continuous management of network performance are crucial for ensuring that a large network operates at peak efficiency. Network performance monitoring tools that provide visibility into metrics such as latency, jitter, bandwidth utilization, and packet loss allow administrators to identify performance degradation before it affects users. Real-time monitoring also enables proactive management of network resources, ensuring that performance bottlenecks are detected and addressed before they lead to major issues. Traffic analysis tools, such as NetFlow or sFlow, can provide detailed insights into traffic patterns, helping administrators fine-tune routing, QoS, and congestion management strategies to maintain optimal performance.

As networks grow in size, performance tuning becomes an ongoing process. What works well for a small network might not be sufficient as the network scales. By continuously monitoring network performance, optimizing routing protocols, implementing traffic engineering strategies, and fine-tuning security mechanisms, network engineers can ensure that large networks remain efficient, stable, and responsive to the needs of the organization. The key to success in performance tuning is a holistic approach, considering every aspect of the network and constantly adapting to changing traffic patterns and organizational requirements.

Chapter 49: Lab Design and Simulation Tools

Lab design and simulation tools are fundamental resources for network engineers, educators, and anyone involved in the configuration, testing, and deployment of network infrastructure. These tools provide an environment for testing new configurations, validating design choices, and troubleshooting network issues before they are implemented in live, production environments. By using simulation and emulation tools, engineers can avoid costly mistakes, optimize designs, and ensure that their networks will function as intended under various conditions. In the world of network engineering, the importance of lab design and simulation tools cannot be overstated as they allow for experimentation and learning without the risks associated with real-world deployment.

The primary advantage of lab design and simulation tools is the ability to model complex networks and simulate their behavior under different conditions. These tools allow users to create virtual network topologies that represent real-world scenarios, complete with routers, switches, firewalls, and other network devices. Engineers can then apply different routing protocols, configure interfaces, and test various protocols in a controlled, isolated environment. This process helps validate assumptions, discover potential issues, and explore multiple configuration scenarios without affecting live network traffic. Additionally, using lab tools enables engineers to practice troubleshooting in a safe environment, preparing them to handle real-world network outages, misconfigurations, or failures effectively.

One of the most popular and widely used simulation tools is Cisco Packet Tracer. Developed by Cisco, this tool provides a graphical interface for simulating network topologies and configurations. Packet Tracer is particularly useful for those studying for Cisco certifications or for educational purposes. It allows users to drag and drop various devices such as routers, switches, and PCs, configure them, and observe how the network operates. Packet Tracer supports a wide range of network protocols including IP, OSPF, EIGRP, BGP, and VLANs. While it has some limitations in terms of advanced features and scalability compared to more professional tools, Packet Tracer remains an excellent entry-level option for network simulation, enabling users to experiment with a variety of configurations and network setups.

Another powerful tool for network simulation is GNS3 (Graphical Network Simulator-3). Unlike Packet Tracer, GNS3 allows users to run real Cisco IOS images, making it a more versatile tool for simulating advanced configurations and network behaviors. GNS3 is used extensively in professional and certification environments, such as for preparing for the CCNP and CCIE exams. One of the key features of GNS3 is its ability to integrate with real devices, which allows users to simulate both virtual and physical devices in a single topology. This hybrid approach makes GNS3 particularly valuable for engineers who need to test configurations that closely mimic real-world conditions.

Additionally, GNS3 supports a wide range of network devices from different vendors, such as Juniper and MikroTik, which expands its utility for professionals working in multi-vendor environments.

For more detailed simulations, especially for larger-scale network environments, tools like EVE-NG (Emulated Virtual Environment Next Generation) and Cisco VIRL (Virtual Internet Routing Lab) provide even more advanced features. These tools offer the capability to emulate entire data center environments, including virtual routers, switches, and firewalls. EVE-NG, for example, supports a variety of devices from multiple vendors, making it a highly versatile tool for professionals working in heterogeneous network environments. Cisco VIRL, on the other hand, is a more tailored solution designed specifically for Cisco environments, allowing users to run full Cisco IOS and NX-OS images in a virtualized environment. VIRL enables users to create complex network topologies and test configurations with a high degree of accuracy, making it an ideal tool for simulating enterprise-level deployments and validating complex network designs before they are implemented.

Lab design and simulation tools not only help engineers configure and test network devices but also allow for the simulation of network traffic. By creating simulated traffic flows, engineers can observe how the network handles different types of data and identify potential bottlenecks, congestion points, or performance issues. This is particularly useful in large-scale networks where monitoring and troubleshooting performance issues in real time can be challenging. Simulating traffic in a lab environment gives engineers the ability to predict how the network will behave under various load conditions and can help fine-tune configurations for optimal performance.

Network emulation tools go beyond simulation by allowing users to replicate real network conditions, such as latency, jitter, and packet loss. This feature is crucial for testing Quality of Service (QoS) configurations, VoIP setups, and other latency-sensitive applications. For instance, tools like WANem (Wide Area Network Emulator) can emulate WAN conditions such as bandwidth restrictions, packet loss, and delay. This allows network engineers to test how well their networks handle different traffic types under challenging conditions, such as limited bandwidth or intermittent connectivity. Emulation tools are vital for preparing a network for real-world usage, ensuring that engineers can account for the variability and unpredictability of the production environment.

In addition to simulation and emulation, lab design tools also help network engineers plan and document network topologies. With tools like Microsoft Visio, engineers can create detailed network diagrams that represent physical and logical network layouts. These diagrams provide a visual representation of the network's design, helping engineers communicate their design choices, plan for future expansions, and document the current state of the network. Network design tools are especially useful for large-scale projects where many devices and configurations must be coordinated across different teams and departments. Clear documentation is essential for maintaining an organized network and ensuring that changes can be easily tracked and managed over time.

For troubleshooting, lab design and simulation tools provide an invaluable resource for engineers to practice diagnosing and resolving network issues. By recreating real-world failure scenarios in a controlled lab environment, engineers can improve their troubleshooting skills and learn how to resolve issues efficiently. This hands-on experience can significantly reduce the time it takes to identify and fix problems in a live network. Tools like Wireshark and tcpdump can be used to capture network traffic during simulations, allowing engineers to analyze the flow of packets and detect issues such as misconfigured IP addresses, routing loops, or security vulnerabilities.

The ability to simulate and test network configurations and designs before implementation allows engineers to identify potential issues early and avoid costly mistakes. By using lab design and simulation tools, engineers can develop a deeper understanding of how network protocols interact, how different devices respond to changes, and how to optimize configurations for performance and scalability. These tools empower network professionals to create, test, and refine network designs that are both efficient and reliable, ensuring that the final deployment meets the needs of the organization and its users. The use of these tools continues to grow as networks become more complex and demanding, making lab design and simulation an indispensable part of network engineering practice.

Chapter 50: Interview Questions and Certification Tips

In the field of network engineering, whether pursuing a career or advancing one, both job interviews and certification exams are significant milestones. These processes serve as a means to evaluate knowledge, skills, and experience, while also offering opportunities for growth and career progression. For network professionals, understanding the most common interview questions and preparing for certification exams is essential for both securing positions and demonstrating expertise in a competitive industry. Preparing for these scenarios involves not only technical knowledge but also an understanding of how to present oneself effectively, highlight relevant skills, and stay up to date with the latest developments in networking technologies.

Job interviews for network engineers often begin with a discussion of the candidate's technical expertise. Common interview questions focus on basic networking concepts, such as OSI and TCP/IP models, IP addressing, subnetting, routing protocols, and network security. These foundational concepts serve as the backbone for understanding more complex systems and protocols. Interviewers might ask about the differences between IPv4 and IPv6, the purpose of subnet masks, or how to configure and troubleshoot routers and switches. Expect to explain the mechanics of routing protocols like OSPF, EIGRP, and BGP, as well as how these protocols are implemented in real-world networks. A strong understanding of routing table entries, path selection algorithms, and the significance of metrics in routing protocols is crucial for demonstrating expertise in the networking field.

Another set of interview questions focuses on troubleshooting and network performance. Employers look for candidates who can effectively diagnose and resolve network issues under pressure. In these interviews, you may be asked to explain how you would approach troubleshooting a network outage or slow connectivity. Questions may include: "How would you diagnose a routing loop?" or "What steps would you take to resolve a network that is experiencing high latency?" These questions evaluate problem-solving skills, familiarity with diagnostic tools like ping, traceroute, and Wireshark, and the ability to methodically approach network failures. It's important to demonstrate a systematic approach to problem-solving, including verifying the physical layer, checking routing tables, and inspecting device configurations.

Security-related interview questions are also common in networking roles. With cyber threats becoming more sophisticated, employers are increasingly looking for candidates who can secure network infrastructures. You might be asked to explain how firewalls, VPNs, and intrusion detection/prevention systems work and how they are configured to protect network resources. Questions about securing BGP, preventing routing attacks, and implementing network access control lists (ACLs) are frequently posed in interviews for positions that involve network security responsibilities. Interviewers may also ask about your experience with securing protocols such as HTTPS, SSH, or SNMPv3, as well as your approach to encryption and authentication methods like IPsec and SSL/TLS.

In addition to technical questions, interviewers will likely ask about your experience with network design and implementation. This could involve describing past projects where you designed or managed network topologies, configured large-scale routing implementations, or handled complex interconnectivity between different network segments. You may be asked to discuss how you would design a scalable, redundant, and fault-tolerant network for a growing company or how you would troubleshoot network performance in such a design. This gives interviewers insight into your practical experience with real-world scenarios and your ability to work within the constraints and objectives of an organization's specific needs.

When preparing for certifications, it is essential to understand the specific exam objectives for the certification you are pursuing. Cisco's CCNA, CCNP, and CCIE exams, as well as other vendor-specific certifications, are structured around both theoretical and hands-on skills. The CCNA exam, for example, covers a broad range of topics, including network fundamentals, security fundamentals, automation, IP addressing, and routing protocols. Candidates preparing for CCNA certification should focus on understanding basic network architectures, configuring routers and switches, and troubleshooting simple networks. A solid grasp of subnetting and the ability to quickly perform subnet calculations is often a key component of success in certification exams.

For more advanced certifications like the CCNP and CCIE, candidates must demonstrate a deeper understanding of complex networking concepts and advanced troubleshooting techniques. These exams typically include scenario-based questions that require you to apply your knowledge to real-world network designs and troubleshooting situations. You will be tested on the configuration of advanced routing protocols, quality of service (QoS) mechanisms, network security, and multicast routing. To prepare for these exams, candidates should engage in hands-on practice with networking equipment or virtual lab environments such as GNS3 or Cisco Packet Tracer. These platforms offer the ability to create lab environments that simulate real-world networks, enabling candidates to practice and reinforce their theoretical knowledge.

One of the most effective ways to prepare for these certifications is to leverage study guides, video tutorials, and practice exams. Study guides provide a structured approach to covering all the exam topics and can help you identify areas where you need additional review. Practice exams allow you to assess your knowledge and become familiar with the format of the exam. These tools also help you manage your time and increase your confidence by familiarizing you with the types of questions you will face on the actual exam day. For hands-on preparation, creating and configuring network topologies in a lab setting is invaluable. Experimenting with real equipment or virtualized devices in a safe, controlled environment helps reinforce concepts and provides a deeper understanding of how networking protocols work in practice.

Networking certifications, while essential for validating skills, also provide networking professionals with the credibility needed to advance in their careers. Employers often require certifications as a way of ensuring that candidates possess the requisite technical skills and knowledge to handle the challenges of managing large-scale networks. In addition to certifications, experience plays a significant role in the interview process. As such, having a solid portfolio of practical experience, including internships, previous job roles, or personal projects, is a critical advantage. During interviews, being able to speak to specific scenarios, challenges, and solutions you've worked on demonstrates not only your theoretical understanding but also your ability to apply that knowledge in a real-world context.

Interviewing for network engineering positions and preparing for certifications requires a combination of theoretical understanding, hands-on practice, and effective communication skills. Being able to discuss your technical expertise in routing, security, troubleshooting, and network design is essential. Certification exams will test your depth of knowledge, but interviews often emphasize the ability to think critically, solve complex problems, and communicate effectively. Whether you are just starting your career or seeking to advance in the networking field, having a comprehensive study plan, practical experience, and the ability to showcase your skills in interviews will increase your chances of success.

Chapter 51: Future of Dynamic Routing Protocols

The future of dynamic routing protocols is one of evolution, where existing protocols continue to adapt to meet the demands of modern networks while new concepts and innovations emerge to address the challenges of a highly interconnected and increasingly complex digital world. As the networking landscape continues to evolve with the expansion of the Internet of Things (IoT), cloud computing, data center virtualization, and 5G networks, the need for more flexible, scalable, and intelligent routing solutions is becoming more pronounced. Dynamic routing protocols like OSPF, EIGRP, and BGP have been the backbone of network routing for decades, but they must evolve to handle the demands of emerging technologies and the growing scale of global networks.

One of the key trends in the future of dynamic routing is the integration of machine learning (ML) and artificial intelligence (AI) into routing protocols. As networks become more complex, managing them with traditional static configurations and human intervention is no longer sufficient. ML and AI have the potential to revolutionize how routing decisions are made, enabling networks to adapt to changes in real time based on performance data and traffic patterns. For instance, AI could be used to predict network congestion or identify the best path based on dynamic conditions, such as user behavior, application requirements, and external factors like weather or traffic load. This could lead to networks that are not only more efficient but also self-optimizing, able to adjust routing parameters on the fly to ensure optimal performance.

Another significant development in the future of dynamic routing is the increased use of automation and intent-based networking. Traditional network configurations are often complex and manually intensive, requiring significant time and expertise to configure and maintain. Automation tools, such as Ansible, Puppet, and Chef, are already being used to automate the deployment and management of network devices and configurations. In the future, these automation tools will likely be integrated into routing protocols, enabling networks to automatically adjust their routing tables and paths based on defined policies or business intents. Intent-based networking allows network administrators to define high-level goals or policies, such as ensuring low latency for video conferencing or optimizing traffic for cloud applications, and the network can automatically implement the best routing strategy to achieve those goals. This will not only simplify network management but also make networks more responsive to business needs.

In parallel with automation and AI, the evolution of software-defined networking (SDN) is another significant driver of change for dynamic routing protocols. SDN separates the control plane from the data plane, providing centralized control over the entire network. This paradigm allows for more granular control over routing decisions, enabling administrators to dynamically adjust traffic flows based on network conditions, user requirements, or application priorities. SDN will likely result in the development of new routing protocols designed specifically for programmable networks, enabling faster and more efficient routing decisions. These protocols will need to be highly flexible, capable of adjusting in real time to shifting traffic patterns and network topologies, and they will likely work in conjunction with AI and automation tools to ensure optimal routing in a dynamic environment.

As the use of cloud services continues to expand, dynamic routing protocols will also need to adapt to the increasing reliance on virtualized and distributed infrastructures. Cloud providers are building massive data centers that rely on virtualized networks, and traffic patterns in these environments can be highly dynamic, with workloads moving between servers or even across geographic locations in real time. Traditional routing protocols like BGP, which were designed for static IP addresses and predictable routing paths, will need to evolve to handle this level of mobility. New protocols or enhancements to existing protocols may emerge to better support traffic distribution in virtualized environments, ensuring that data flows efficiently across cloud networks while maintaining high availability and low latency.

5G and the growing adoption of IoT devices are also shaping the future of dynamic routing. With the proliferation of connected devices and the demand for ultra-low latency and high bandwidth, traditional routing protocols may struggle to keep up with the scale and speed required by 5G networks. Dynamic routing protocols will need to be more intelligent and efficient in handling the vast amount of data generated by billions of IoT devices. This may require protocols that are capable of quickly adapting to changes in network topologies and can prioritize traffic based on the criticality of the application. For example, in smart cities or autonomous vehicle networks, routing protocols will need to prioritize safety-related traffic over other data streams to ensure timely communication in critical situations. The future of dynamic routing will thus involve protocols that can handle a wide variety of traffic types and prioritize them accordingly.

One of the most important considerations for the future of dynamic routing is security. As the number of connected devices increases and networks become more interconnected, the risk of security breaches also grows. BGP, for example, has long been a target for attacks such as BGP hijacking and route leaks, which can lead to traffic interception or network outages. To address these vulnerabilities, future dynamic routing protocols will likely incorporate more robust security mechanisms, such as stronger encryption, authentication, and validation methods. The integration of blockchain technology into routing protocols is one possibility that could provide a more secure and tamper-resistant method of verifying routing information. Blockchain's decentralized and immutable ledger could be used to verify the authenticity of BGP routes, preventing attacks and ensuring the integrity of routing data.

The growing demand for real-time traffic analysis and monitoring will also influence the evolution of dynamic routing protocols. In the future, routing protocols will need to be capable of collecting and analyzing vast amounts of network data in real time to make more informed routing decisions. This could include data on network performance, security threats, and application behavior, allowing protocols to adjust routing paths dynamically based on this information. Real-time analytics will also help network operators identify issues before they become critical, enabling proactive maintenance and improving the overall reliability of the network.

In the coming years, the future of dynamic routing protocols will be characterized by more adaptive, intelligent, and automated systems. Machine learning, AI, SDN, and cloud computing will continue to shape the landscape of network routing, making networks more responsive to changing conditions and business needs. The protocols themselves will evolve to be more flexible, scalable, and secure, capable of handling the challenges posed by new technologies like 5G and IoT. As the networking landscape continues to grow in complexity, dynamic routing protocols will become more integrated with other network management tools, creating highly efficient and self-optimizing networks that can handle the demands of an increasingly digital world. The future of dynamic routing promises to be an exciting and transformative chapter in the history of networking.

www.ingramcontent.com/pod-product-compliance
Lightning Source LLC
LaVergne TN
LVHW051236050326
832903LV00028B/2434